Internet
research skills

Internet
research skills

Niall Ó Dochartaigh | third edition

Los Angeles | London | New Delhi
Singapore | Washington DC

Los Angeles | London | New Delhi
Singapore | Washington DC

SAGE Publications Ltd
1 Oliver's Yard
55 City Road
London EC1Y 1SP

SAGE Publications Inc.
2455 Teller Road
Thousand Oaks, California 91320

SAGE Publications India Pvt Ltd
B 1/I 1 Mohan Cooperative Industrial Area
Mathura Road
New Delhi 110 044

SAGE Publications Asia-Pacific Pte Ltd
3 Church Street
#10-04 Samsung Hub
Singapore 049483

Editor: Katie Metzler
Editorial assistant: Anna Horvai
Production editor: Ian Antcliff
Copyeditor: Sarah Bury
Proofreader: Kate Harrison
Marketing manager: Ben Griffin-Sherwood
Cover design: Lisa Harper
Typeset by: C&M Digitals (P) Ltd
Printed and bound by CPI group (UK) Ltd,
Croydon, CRO 4YY

© 2012 Niall Ó Dochartaigh
© 2012 Chapter 7 Niall Ó Dochartaigh and Patricia Sleeman

First edition published 2001; second edition 2007.
This edition 2012

Library of Congress Control Number: 2011939245

British Library Cataloguing in Publication data

A catalogue record for this book is available from
the British Library

ISBN 978-0-85702-528-9
ISBN 978-0-85702-529-6 (pbk)

Contents

Figures and Tables

Figures

Tables

Chapter 5

Chapter 8

List of Boxes

About the author

Niall Ó Dochartaigh is the author of *From Civil Rights to Armalites: Derry and the Birth of the Irish Troubles* (Cork UP 1997; Palgrave 2004) and two books on internet research (Sage 2002; 2007). He has published extensively on conflict, negotiation, territory and new technologies in a range of journals including the *Journal of Peace Research, Political Geography, The International Journal of Conflict Management, Irish Political Studies, Mobilization, Identities, The Field Day Review* and *Contemporary British History*. His current research analyses secret communication between the British government and the IRA in the Northern Ireland conflict. He has been a visiting scholar at the University of California, Berkeley; the Annenberg School for Communication, USC; the University of Auckland and the University of Otago. He is convener of the specialist group on Peace and Conflict of the Political Studies Association of Ireland. He is a college lecturer in the School of Political Science and Sociology at the National University of Ireland, Galway. Further information is available at niallodoc.wordpress.com.

Acknowledgements

Thanks to Carol-Ann for providing good advice over many months. Mo Bhuíochas le Caoimhe agus Dara chomh maith.

Thanks especially to Peter Murphy, Elizabeth Ball and Aogán Mulcahy, who read and made comments on all or most of the draft, and to Niall Ó Murchú. Thanks to Katie Metzler and to Anna Horvai at Sage for helping to steer this edition to completion. Thanks also to Patrick Brindle at Sage for providing encouragement and useful advice on the previous edition of this book.

Thanks also to Jonathan Heaney, Carol Staunton, Katy Hayward, Daniel Savery, Lorenzo Bosi, Su-Ming Khoo, Gwen Ryan, Niall Ó Cíosáin, Bernard Ryan, Brendan Flynn and John Canavan.

ONE

Introduction

Into the cloud: new research skills
for the information age

The term 'cloud computing' was coined several years ago to refer to the practice of storing and working with data and documents in an online 'cloud' that draws on multiple connected computers. It's also a good metaphor for the Internet and for the new information environment in which we are all now operating. We are enveloped in information, and saturated by it. To a certain extent we are blinded by it. The sheer volume of information can obscure our vision and hinder understanding. The task of identifying what is reliable, what is ground-breaking and, above all else, what is important becomes more challenging as the volume of information increases. Several recent books argue that the problems generated by the onrush of new information technologies present a radically new challenge to the pursuit of knowledge and understanding. *Is Google making us stupid?*, a recent article later expanded into a book called *The Shallows* (Carr, 2010), argues that the use of the Internet is changing the way we absorb information and consequently changing the way we think. Emphasizing the way in which the technology allows us to move rapidly between bite-sized chunks of information, the author argues that we are losing the skills necessary to absorb and understand long and complex sets of information. A whole raft of recent books with titles like *Distracted* (Jackson, 2009), *The Overflowing Brain* (Klingberg, 2009), *Grown up Digital* (Tapscott, 2009) and, perhaps most provocatively, *The Dumbest Generation*, subtitled *How the digital age stupefies young Americans and jeopardizes our future* (Bauerlein, 2008), make related points, arguing that we are in the midst of a deep historical shift in the way in which we absorb information and the way in which we think. While the sense of panic, crisis and impending Internet doom may be a little overdone at times, it is nonetheless clear that researchers face radically new challenges. In this new environment, the most important research skills relate to channelling, evaluating, selecting and restricting information rather than the simple assembling of large quantities of related information.

The foundational authors of the modern social sciences and humanities, writing between the late eighteenth century and the early twentieth century, worked in a context in which an academic researcher and writer could still acquire something close to a comprehensive knowledge of a relatively broad field or topic and could hope to read 'everything' on their subject. They hungrily sought out new perspectives from other fields too. Sigmund Freud's foundational work *The Interpretation of Dreams*, first published in 1900, provides a clear illustration of the importance attached by those early writers to a comprehensive approach to reading and research. The book begins with a brief literature survey in which Freud traced the way in which dreams have been understood and analyzed back to Aristotle and the first written references to dreams in the texts of ancient Greece. His survey stretched across a wide range of disciplines too. While Freud stressed that the existing work on dreams was too extensive even then for him to attempt to survey it comprehensively, the comprehensiveness of his ambition is evident. He wanted to make sure he hadn't left out any significant source, that he hadn't missed a relevant reference, no matter what discipline it originated in.

By the middle of the twentieth century the explosive growth in academic research and publication had generated such monumental volumes of research that the aspiration to comprehensive knowledge of even a major sub-section of a particular literature was moving beyond the reach of any single individual. The term 'information overload' entered common parlance in the 1970s, long before the Internet existed. A variety of factors associated with the new technologies have generated an exponential growth in research publications over the past 20 years. Where the core task of the researcher of the early twentieth century was to seek out and retrieve every possible significant reference to, and study of, their topic, a core task of the twenty-first-century researcher is to limit, to restrict and to channel the flows of information effectively.

We can draw a useful analogy here with changing levels of accessibility to resources of a different kind. Information is not the only field in which there has been an exponential growth in choice and a consequent emphasis on the importance of quality assessment, limitation and restriction in recent decades. After several millennia in which the central human struggle was to kill or grow or gather enough food to sustain life, the over-abundance and easy accessibility of food in prosperous countries during the past half-century has entirely reversed some key elements of the human relationship to food. The rotund figure of the medieval king, his fatness a symbol of prosperity and abundance, has given way to images of slender power that celebrate restrictive eating habits and self-control.

The most important central strategies relating to nutrition in prosperous coun-tries are now directed at restricting the intake of food, and managing that intake much more self-consciously. In an analogous way, researchers have found it nec-essary to adapt to the seemingly limitless cloud of information by bounding and limiting and restricting their reading and their information intake much more tightly than before. The ability to find 'something' on a topic, or to find huge volumes of material on a topic, has diminished in importance while the ability to sift through these huge volumes and identify small numbers of key sources and texts has become a core skill. Now more than ever, researchers need to develop information-searching skills and an expertise in their subject area that allows them to identify and highlight the critical central resources in their research area. Increasingly, that also involves building networks with others in the same field and drawing on their experience and shared knowledge.

The rise of the search engines

The big keyword search engines such as Google and its academic offshoot Google Scholar are now at the centre of the research process. Alternative approaches to finding resources modelled on traditional library classification schemes have proved unviable. A decade and a half of library and academic efforts to stem the rise of Google as a research tool and promote alternative searching approaches through the systematic cataloguing and organizing of online academic resources by subject area is drawing to a close. This vast decentralized project, embarked on in the 1990s by a variety of different initiatives and institutions, attempted to replicate the role of libraries in cataloguing and organizing books by subject and sub-topic to help students and researchers to find the materials they needed. It has now been almost completely abandoned. A key milestone was passed in 2011 when the UK's large and carefully maintained academic subject catalogue, Intute, finally ran out of hope and resources, and shut down (Chapter 4). However, increased reliance on the big search engines is not without its problems. The scattershot approach to online research that they facilitate provides a large part of the explanation for the rapid rise in student use of poor quality and unreliable sources in recent years. In a 2004 survey of over 2,300 US university professors, over 42 per cent said that the quality of student work had worsened with use of the Internet. Only 22 per cent thought it had improved (Jones and Johnson-Yale, 2005). The big search engines will remain at the centre of the research process, however, and there will be no return to the library as the main source of reading for the vast majority of students and academic researchers.

The scrupulously careful and systematic cataloguers were outflanked on two sides. On the one hand, the keyword search engines, chief among them Google, have become steadily more sophisticated, guessing what we want even as we type it, drawing on our previous search patterns to identify the kinds of resources we might be interested in, and bringing central resources to the top of their results lists. If you have an established pattern of searching for academic research resources in a particular subject area, the search engine modifies your query accordingly to bring these kinds of resources to the top of your search results. It becomes increasingly difficult to justify the time spent browsing through a catalogue of websites when a keyword search engine is now likely to pull up many of the same sites more quickly.

Searching by keyword has won out over the big cataloguing projects but searching by subject is not dead. It has just taken on a new form; more specialized, more personalized and more diffuse. The big catalogues were outflanked on one side by keyword search engines, but on the other side they have been overtaken by new methods of organizing material by subject area that generate much more focused and specialized kinds of subject guides, without necessarily using this term. Curricula and reading lists for university courses, for example, act as guides to the literature in very precise sub-fields. They are now more widely available than ever before through a range of open courseware initiatives (Chapter 2). The list of references at the end of any academic article constitutes a different kind of specialized guide to reading on a topic. The seamless linking between academic databases that we now enjoy makes it easy to chase up related reading from an article that is central to our area of interest. It is a subject-searching approach that is simpler and generally more productive than looking for material classified under the same subject heading (Chapter 3). One of the most effective strategies for sensibly restricting your reading is to simply follow the reference trail in your field. Begin by identifying several key publications on your topic, through advice from colleagues, supervisors, instructors and fellow-researchers around you or those connected to you online. Then follow the reference trail forward and backward in time. Look at the list of references for these key works to see what work has been cited by these key authors, then chase up those that relate directly to your research topic. Moving forward in time, search for articles that have subsequently cited the texts that relate most closely to your project, limiting this search with one or two words related to your topic that will help to cut out irrelevant results. You can do both of these kinds of searches in virtually every online service that includes academic research publications. These services are dealt with in detail in the next two chapters. You can then in turn follow the references forward and backward for the most important books and articles that you turn up in these initial searches. In the process of carrying out a search like this you begin to map out the particular field you are working in and to set out the boundaries of your research project.

Social media and 'user-generated content' have also led to a proliferation of new kinds of specialized guides. Resources as varied as academic blogs, Amazon's Listmania (Chapter 2), Facebook and academic networking sites such as **academia.edu** (Chapter 9), eclectically gather together related resources by combining the efforts of networked enthusiasts. With the marginalization and decline of the big subject guides, the keyword search engines and the specialized guides to resources in very precisely defined subject areas, available in many different forms, are now the twin pillars of online searching and research.

Understanding the Internet

The Internet is not an organized system. No one is in charge. It is not primarily a network or even a network of networks. Above all, it's a simple fact – the fact that millions of computers across the world can communicate with each other. When you click a link on your computer screen, your computer sends a message to another computer asking it to send you the file or files that the link refers to. The other computer will understand the request and will send the files. Essentially, the Internet consists of files on other people's computers, including text, audio and video files, that they allow the outside world to look at. To put their information 'on the Internet' people just move a file to that part of their computer, or to another computer, that is open to the outside world.

The networks that carry your request include phone lines, satellite dishes and cables. Such lines of communication have existed for a long time. Many of them were not built specifically to carry Internet traffic and they are not the essence of the Internet.

The Internet has existed since the 1960s. That is, computers have been able to communicate over long distances since then. When the World Wide Web came into existence in 1993 it became far easier for the wider public to take advantage of this fact. The web is based on http, the Hyper Text Transfer Protocol, and the major innovation it introduced was hypertext, the links in web pages that link you to another web page. Embedded in every hyperlink is an Internet address, a URL. It might point you to another document or image on the computer you are connected to or it might point you to a document or image on a computer on the other side of the world. It allowed people to create very elaborate documents online for the first time, including links to other documents, to graphics, to sound and to video.

The web is not to be confused with the information people make available on their computers. Everybody puts up his or her own information. The web 'protocol' just means that all the machines understand each other and display documents from other machines in a standard way. Web browsers such as Safari, Firefox or Internet Explorer are not responsible for that information. They simply provide an easy way to view it.

Summary of chapters

The book begins with two chapters that focus on academic books and articles online, directing users towards the best organized and the most authoritative resources available, before moving on to deal in later chapters with the open

Web online resources outside the big databases that are much less clearly organized and much more difficult to search effectively and to assess. Search strategies illustrated by examples in each chapter combine a variety of online resources in pursuit of a series of research tasks. These strategies bring readers from the initial exploration of their topic, through the literature search, to the identification of major sources, the development of specialized search queries and the search for primary sources of data and documentation. The wide range of online resources drawn on in these strategies emphasize the fact that the big search engines, on which many people rely entirely, provide access to only a fraction of the research resources available online.

Chapter 2 focuses on academic books online. A range of online services, including bookshops such as Amazon and search services such as Google Book Search, provide new ways to access the full text of academic books while e-books allow researchers to annotate, organize and search academic books in new ways. This chapter outlines strategies for combining different online resources to conduct the kind of book searches that were impossible a few years ago, using online library catalogues, publisher websites and online course materials. It outlines the way in which 'needle in the haystack' searches can now direct you to books that you would never have been alerted to through their title or list of contents, how to use these services to identify key works in your area and how to incorporate novel resources, such as reader reviews, into your search strategies.

Chapter 3 deals primarily with academic articles. It explains how to combine the databases of abstracts, full text databases, library catalogues, Google Scholar and similar tools to make full use of the available resources. It explains the extent to which these services overlap and the ways in which they differ, explaining their comparative strengths and weaknesses and untangling the overlapping content of competing companies. It assesses the commercial databases devoted to particular subject areas and emphasizes the value of review articles. It deals too with the increased access to articles, theses, dissertations, working papers, conference papers and other kinds of academic material that have been made possible through the open access movement and the growth of institutional repositories.

Chapter 4 is the first chapter to deal with the 'open Web', a realm of chaos in comparison with the databases of academic books and articles. It outlines approaches to dealing with an information environment in which the authorship and reliability of resources is often unclear and resources are much less clearly organized, structured and bounded than in the databases of journal articles and books. It discusses guides to academic resources online that organize materials by subject area and outlines strategies for identifying the key online resources in your area. It describes how websites are organized, explaining enough about the technology to allow readers to develop a better understanding of the materials they are looking at and the context in which these materials are located.

The big keyword search engines such as Google, Yahoo and Bing are dealt with in Chapter 5. The chapter discusses the implications of the intensifying customization of search results for individual researchers. It discusses advanced search options, provides advice on analyzing results, explains how and what the search engines search and provides advice on building queries. It explains how to make effective and efficient use of these search engines.

Web 2.0 and Web 3.0 are the terms used to describe a new generation of online services and resources characterized in part by their interactive nature. Many of these services blur the distinction between writer and reader, producer and consumer, incorporating the contributions of viewers and readers into online services to create powerful and novel means of classifying and locating information. Chapter 6 on 'Social media, news and multimedia' deals with these services, with news sources and with a range of visual and audio resources available online.

Chapter 7 considers government sources, archives and statistics. Perhaps the most dramatic effect of the new technologies has been to open up access to these primary sources, allowing us to search millions of pages of legislative debates, to access not only statistical reports but in many cases the raw data on which they are based as well, and to make archives much more transparent. This chapter identifies key resources for searching these primary sources and suggests strategies for approaching them.

Chapter 8 sets out detailed guidelines for evaluating and understanding online sources, providing a set of questions that can usefully be asked of any materials found online. It also provides detailed advice on citing a variety of online materials.

The book ends with a chapter that provides advice on organizing your research and managing your research notes and readings. It compares a variety of reference management packages and weighs up the benefits and drawbacks of pouring all of your research references into a particular software package. It deals too with the online networks that link together postgraduate students and researchers, discussing the most recent developments and services that are specifically devoted to academic networking. Finally, it provides a brief survey of online research methods, many of them used by researchers who are currently exploring the Internet itself as a site of social change and political activism. It looks too at the new kinds of data about social change that are being generated by online searching and interaction and at how researchers are beginning to use this data to address both old and new questions about the nature of the social and the political.

This book focuses primarily on English-language resources, and on multilingual resources that include the English language. In every language there will be a range of additional key resources uniquely important to those searching for resources in that language but they are beyond the scope of this book.

Who this book is aimed at

This book is intended as a textbook for courses on Internet research skills both at undergraduate and postgraduate level, courses that introduce students in the humanities and social sciences to efficient and critical use of the Internet as a research resource. It will also be of use to researchers in a wide range of areas, from media to government to the voluntary sector, who are concerned with issues of current debate and controversy. The book assumes that the reader makes regular, if sometimes unproductive and frustrating, use of the Internet for research.

It will be useful to advanced undergraduates writing an extended essay or pursuing an independent research assignment for the first time, particularly if they hope to continue to postgraduate level. It is aimed particularly at postgraduate students embarking on a thesis or dissertation. It is an ideal companion to the first year of a PhD thesis when a student is writing a literature review, exploring the field and identifying major resources. The book provides focused advice on a range of tasks involved in writing a thesis or dissertation, and associated exercises.

The book will also be valuable to experienced researchers who make regular use of the Internet but who have never systematically explored the resources available in their area and have never developed systematic strategies for carrying out online research.

The exercises at the end of each chapter bring readers through the material covered in the text while allowing them the freedom to concentrate on their own area of research or special interest. By simply doing the exercises readers will work their way steadily through many of the central tasks involved in their own research project. Throughout the book the importance of taking a critical approach to sources and the need to develop a better understanding of online sources are emphasized.

The book will help all readers to organize their online research, to identify major resources in their areas, to flexibly combine a variety of online resources in the pursuit of specific tasks, to use the big search engines more effectively and efficiently, to critically evaluate online resources, and to take much fuller advantage of the huge potential of online resources in their own research.

TWO

Books

Print publications online

The Internet and the printed word are sometimes discussed as though they were two distinct kinds of information, one of them unreliable and suspect, the other dependable and trustworthy. Over the past few years this distinction has broken down completely and it no longer makes any sense to think of the Internet and the printed word as two opposing categories. After a decade of rapid technological and economic change, the Internet is now the main medium for distributing and accessing articles from academic journals, and it is fast becoming a principal medium for distributing and accessing books. If you're looking for print publications, the best place to start is online.

Although the distinction between what is online and what is in print is breaking down, the concept of print publication continues to be important. Online documents that are also available in print form have generally gone through a set of quality control measures which have developed in the world of print publishing, measures which the bulk of purely online documents do not have to go through. Print publications are much more likely to have gone through a peer review process, whereby people with expertise in the field assess whether they are worth publishing, through an editing process in which authors are encouraged to improve their work, and through copy-editing and proof-reading processes aimed at eliminating errors. These processes are far from flawless and are the subject of much harsh and justified criticism (Harley and Acord, 2011). Print publications can be poorly written, error laden and biased just like web pages, even when they have been through peer review. Decisions on what to publish are often bound up with academic power struggles, fads and fashions and complex personal networks. The essential point here is that you have to approach any piece of writing with a critical eye, regardless of the source.

Nonetheless, print publications online constitute a distinctive genre of document that is marked out from other online materials that are not subject to the same quality-control processes. They constitute the most clearly organized and quality controlled sector of the online world and they remain the single most important online resource for anyone doing research in the social sciences or the humanities. When you are writing on a research topic, you are expected to address the central debates and the established body of knowledge around this topic in the academic literature. For this reason alone it is important that you start your research with the online services devoted to academic books and articles.

Order and chaos

In one sense, the world of print online is the best organized and ordered part of the Internet, with texts carefully selected, catalogued, indexed and stored in elaborate databases that allow sophisticated searches. In another sense, it is the most chaotic and confusing part of the Net. These texts have such high commercial value that competing information providers offer multiple routes to overlapping but distinctive databases of these texts. The publishers who own copyright on these publications make deals with a variety of indexing services in order to publicize and sell the materials through as many avenues as possible. Thus a single journal article may be listed in dozens of different databases. To take just one example, articles from *Social History*, a journal located at the intersection between the social sciences and the humanities, are indexed in more than 20 different databases. This is further complicated by the fact that these databases often index journals from different starting points so that one database will cover a journal from 1994 while another will have coverage dating back to 1984. In addition, each database may allow slightly different kinds of search. While there is huge overlap between the databases, it is far from complete and there is no single database you can rely on for comprehensive coverage. It's necessary to search a few if you are trying to make sure you have covered everything in a specialized area. To complicate matters further, you will find that many of the same databases are made available through several different commercial products, all bundling a different selection of databases together to market an all-in-one package.

Access costs

Most of the material in most of the services dealt with below will only be available to you if your university or library pays the subscription fees. Your institution will only subscribe to a selection of the services below. Many services will recognize that you are accessing the service from a computer at your home institution and will automatically give you access via their home page if your institution is subscribed. If this is not the case, you need to check on your university or library's web pages for a link to these services.

Two developments are making life easier for those whose institutions are not subscribed to some of these massive and expensive services. In the first place, more and more databases are allowing anyone to conduct searches of the databases free of charge, while limiting access to full text to subscribers. As search services, they are useful in their own right in identifying material. Several of these services, and a range of new services emerging to cater to the needs of individual researchers, allow you to purchase single articles, although the charges for individual academic articles remain very high. In addition, some services are experimenting with other innovative pricing models which cater to the individual researcher, including the option to buy access to the full contents of a database for a set period of time, an hour or two, or a day perhaps.

Alongside this, there has recently been a significant increase in the volume of freely available academic literature and some of the services below are primarily devoted to distributing this free literature. Despite this, the bulk of high-quality academic literature is locked up in these subscription databases and your access will be very much determined by the amount of hard cash your institution is paying to ensure that you get access to these materials. Increasing numbers of students are bypassing these restrictions by downloading scanned academic books from file-sharing sites.

Some professional associations and research institutes collect together syllabi in their subject areas and make them available online. The Syllabi Initiative of the Society for Historians of American Foreign Relations (**www.shafr.org/teaching/higher-education/syllabi-initiative/**), for example, provides dozens of syllabi online. The American Political Science Association has also put together an extensive list of online syllabi on a range of politics topics (**www.apsanet.org/content_3807.cfm**) and a list of other collections of syllabi online, while the Economic History Association has created an extensive EH.net course syllabi collection (**eh.net/coursesyllabi**). The websites of H-Net discussion lists in the humanities and social sciences (**www.h-net.org**) can be an excellent source of bibliographies and syllabi if there is a list in your subject area.

If a professional association in your subject area has done something similar, it should be your first port of call. Syllabi and reading lists are not as freely available online as they were a few years ago. Many universities that once made materials freely available now use educational software packages that only permit access to students who are registered on the courses. These resources are invisible to the Internet search engines and closed to the public. On the other hand, several major new services have emerged to provide expanded public access to some of these materials.

Jorum (**www.jorum.ac.uk**) This is a UK academic service that provides a massive collection of high-quality course materials that have been uploaded by academics teaching in UK universities. It includes extensive reading lists and syllabi and much more besides. Many of the resources are only available if you are based at an educational institution in the UK.

The Open Course Ware Consortium (**ocwconsortium.org**) This includes a growing number of universities (mainly in the USA) that provide huge collections of syllabi and other course materials online, including videos of all of the lectures for certain courses. You can do a joint search of materials for over 50,000 courses at the OCW site. You can also search the OCW sites of the individual institutions, such as the Massachusetts Institute of Technology (**ocw.mit.edu/index.htm**) and the University of Notre Dame (**ocw.nd.edu**).

Search strategy

Identifying key texts through reading lists

The first step in a literature search is to identify some of the key texts in the area, the works that everyone writing on this area has to engage with because their arguments set the terms of the debate. Your supervisor, professor or lecturer should be a good starting point for information on key texts.

Beyond this, you can also get access to lists of key works in the course syllabi and reading lists made available online by hundreds of thousands of other professors and lecturers. Not every syllabus includes a reading list but most of them do. If you find that your research topic is the subject of an entire course, or forms a major component of a course at another university, the syllabus for that course can be extremely useful, not only in providing a specialized list of key works in the area, but also in the short summaries of topics which are often provided. These can give you a flavour of the key debates in the area. If you are teaching a course of your own, the syllabi of others can provoke ideas and provide useful templates for structuring a course. To search for syllabi on the open Web through a search engine like Google or Yahoo it can often be effective to search using the title of the course and the word syllabus, if it is a commonly taught subject that tends to have the same title across institutions and jurisdictions. Thus a search on **syllabus "social geography"** turns up multiple syllabi on the topic in the first ten hits alone. To retrieve syllabi from a particular country limit your search by domain, to **.edu** for US universities or **.ac.uk** for British universities, for example. An alternative is to search for a key text specific to your topic. If you wanted to do research on the sociology of food, for example, you might do a search on *The Sociology of Food* by Mennell, Murcott and van Otterloo, a key text on the topic. A search in Google on **Syllabus Otterloo "Sociology of Food"** brings back several relevant results, among them syllabi for courses on the 'Sociology of Food and Eating' and 'Food & Drink in the Ancient Mediterranean'. These syllabi provide a list of topics dealt with and a short list of readings.

Some academic disciplines are organized very differently in different countries and non-US researchers may need to find out what subject headings their area of interest comes under in the USA if they are to locate useful American reading lists.

Books and articles

Just as the distinction between print and the Internet is breaking down, so too is the distinction between book and article and paragraph. Increasingly, publishers are bundling books together into online services which organize, describe and sell access to books by chapter and by page, presenting 20 or 30 related books as a kind of advanced encyclopedia or subject-specific database. Some publishers, such as *Taylor and Francis* (**www.ebookstore.tandf.co.uk**), allow subscribers to create their own books by bundling together bits and pieces from the thousands of books they sell, choosing a chapter here and a paragraph there. Publishers such as *Oxford University Press* (**www.oxfordscholarship.com**) now provide short abstracts describing the contents of individual chapters within books and have opened these abstracts to keyword searches by the big search engines like Google and Yahoo. In treating individual chapters as discrete texts, these services erode the distinction between article and book chapter as both become search results within the big Internet search engines. The technology tends to strip these items out of the context in which they were produced. It is important for researchers to understand that context in order to better understand the content.

Reference sources

Reference books such as dictionaries and encyclopedias are easily broken into bite-sized pieces for consumption online because they are collections of short, discrete items, related through cross-references between entries. Large numbers of specialist encyclopedias in the social sciences, which provide concise introductions to key concepts, key debates and key academic writers, are available online. Some of the entries in these reference sources provide valuable introductions to key texts in very specific areas. They provide a good introduction to unfamiliar concepts and writers as you begin your research.

Several publishers who produce a range of closely related reference sources in the social sciences have bundled these books together into online reference collections, searchable by keyword and subject. Most academic libraries should be subscribed to at least one of the services listed below. Most of these services will allow anyone to search the titles and abstracts to get a sense of what is available, but only make the full text available if your university is subscribed to the service. There is a large overlap between some of these services.

Encyclopaedia Britannica online (**Britannica.com**) One of the best-known general encyclopedias. Some features are available free of charge, including short extracts from entries.

Gale Virtual Reference Library (**www.gale.cengage.com/gvrl**) A vast collection of handbooks and encyclopedias from a large number of academic publishers, including a variety of specialized social science reference works. You can limit your search to books in your subject area and you can export citations.

International Encyclopedia of the Social & Behavioural Sciences (**www.sciencedirect. com/science/referenceworks/0080430767**) This massive work from Elsevier, one of the largest social science publishers, includes almost 4,000 articles and is updated annually. Anyone can browse through abstracts describing the entries, organized alphabetically, but the full text is limited to subscribers. Your institution should provide a direct link if it is subscribed.

Oxford Reference Online (**www.oxfordreference.com**) This includes a collection of several social science encyclopedias which can be searched jointly or individually.

Routledge Reference Resources Online (**www.reference.routledge.com**) This includes a collection of social science reference books, currently covering politics, religion and music but with plans for expansion.

Sage Reference Online (**www.sage-ereference.com/**) Provides online access to their printed encyclopedias and handbooks.

Wikipedia (**www.wikipedia.org**) Strictly speaking, Wikipedia doesn't belong here. It has no print version. It is included here because it has become such an important academic reference source. Like the reference sources dealt with above, Wikipedia organizes material by subject and aspires to comprehensive encyclopedic coverage. Wikipedia entries can be written by anyone and altered by anyone. Although it sounds anarchic, this process has seen the development of powerful, well-written and useful articles on a wide range of academic topics. It provides some invaluable introductions to key concepts, debates and thinkers in the social sciences and the humanities. Wikipedia has been rightly criticized for the fact that many readers edit entries in pursuit of their own agendas and for the consequent inclusion of false material. Despite this, it has huge strengths. You would not expect to use it as a central resource for a piece of academic research, or to cite it as a reliable source, but like an encyclopedia, it frequently gives you a good overview of a topic, identifies key debates and provides pointers to key sources. The disputes that rage on Wikipedia are a useful reminder that knowledge is a site of struggle and contest.

Wikipedia is at its best when it comes to obscure topics and current events that would never be covered by any encyclopedia. It is hard to imagine any other way in which information on these obscure topics could be gathered together in such a concise way and be so easy to locate. Despite Wikipedia's flaws, it is simply too valuable a resource to exclude. No encyclopedia can come close to the level of detail it provides and the dynamism of its content. Unlike the sources listed above, it's free.

Library catalogues

Worldcat

With over 220 million records from the combined library catalogues of more than 72,000 libraries worldwide, Worldcat is a central source of bibliographic information on academic books. It is expanding its capabilities to include reviews and reader commentary. The service has its weaknesses and omissions, and more sophisticated searching is possible in the catalogues of individual libraries, but it is massive. Dominated as it is by academic libraries, it deals with a very different set of books from those catalogued by online bookstores. There is much greater historical depth and it is much more heavily weighted towards academic materials. You can download references from Worldcat but in many cases they have not been entered correctly and you'll need to edit them a little after importing them to a reference management package. They provide a useful guide to downloading references and a blog that keeps users updated on new developments. Look for a link to Worldcat from your library's web pages to avail of the full capabilities of the service or go to **worldcat.org** to avail of a much more limited service that is freely available to everyone.

Yahoo, Google Scholar, Google Books and several other online services now search inside the Worldcat database. The 'library search' link on Google Scholar results will take you to Worldcat information on the book in question. You can perform further searches on Worldcat.org results but you can search more flexibly by searching the full Worldcat database directly through your library's link. Worldcat allows you to search by 'class descriptor' (the subject classification number for the book) and by subject, providing two ways to identify closely related books. If you do a subject search in Worldcat.org you get a page of results that contain less detail and flexibility than the results received when you search Worldcat directly. When you have located the entry for the book you are interested in, choose the 'Libraries Worldwide' link to identify libraries near you that contain the book. This can help to identify a nearby library which has a particularly strong collection in your area of interest and which would be worth visiting, to pore over a large number of books in a short time rather than ordering them by Inter Library Loan. If you identify such a library, you can also go directly to its online catalogue and search by the relevant subject and classification number to identify further books that it might be useful to look at while you're there. It is also useful to do a subject search of the catalogues of universities which are home to a specialized research centre or institute in the area you're working on. They should house a large and specialized collection.

Other library catalogues

LibDex, The Library Index (**www.libdex.com**) Search by keyword or browse by country to find links to the online catalogues of academic and public libraries worldwide.

The US Library of Congress (**www.loc.gov**) The official library serving the US legislature. The advanced search allows you to go beyond the book catalogue and to search their collections of manuscripts.

The British Library (**catalogue.bl.uk**) As a copyright library the British Library is entitled to receive a copy of every book published in Britain or Ireland and consequently has a much wider collection than most. It includes specialized collections.

COPAC (**copac.ac.uk**) This allows you to do a unified search of major university research libraries in Britain and Ireland, by subject and by author or title. You can also search it for journals to see which libraries hold the journals you want.

Books in Print (**www.booksinprint.com**) Not strictly speaking a catalogue, university librarians and bookshops use this comprehensive guide to books both in and out of print as an authoritative source of information when buying books. It differs from Worldcat in that its primary focus is on making it possible to buy books. It also allows you to search for audio and video. You can sign up to their alert service which will send you an email when new books matching your interests are added to the database. Select 'forthcoming' to search for books that haven't yet been published. It is only available if your institution subscribes.

Search strategy

Searching by subject in library catalogues

At the early stages of your literature search you can use online library catalogues to identify closely related books. Search for a key text in Worldcat, one that relates to your specific area of interest rather than to the broad subject area. Then choose 'class descriptors' to return a list of books catalogued under the same classification number, belonging to precisely the same area of specialization as the key text. You can also call up a list of books that have been given the same subject descriptor or relate to the same geographic area.

To search for books on gender and sexuality in Victorian Britain, for example, begin by searching Worldcat for a much-cited text, such as *City of Dreadful Delight: Narratives of Sexual Danger in Late-Victorian London* by Judith Walkowitz. The Worldcat entry for the book includes a list of subject categories. Of the half dozen categories into which the book has been placed, one of them clearly fits closely with the research topic of gender and sexuality in Victorian Britain: 'Sex role – England – History – 19th century'. There are 73 items catalogued under this heading, including 54 books. Among the first ten books are several titles that are clearly relevant, including:

- *Limited livelihoods: gender and class in nineteenth-century England*
- *Banishing the beast: sexuality and the early feminists*
- *A man's place: masculinity and the middle-class home in Victorian England*
- *Gender in English society, 1650–1850: the emergence of separate spheres?*

You can use the same strategy to search for books by subject in your own library catalogue. You can also access Worldcat via Google Scholar. Search for the book (using the author surname and the first part of the title). Then click on the 'library search' link for the book. This brings you directly to the Worldcat entry for the book, including the list of subject categories. When you click on 'Sex role – England – History – 19th century' you get a list of all the other books in Worldcat classified under this heading but it differs from the result generated by the Worldcat database, generating 128 results. It appears to include duplicates that are not included in the Worldcat database results.

All 30	Books ◆ 25	Internet ⊕ 3	Visual 📷 1	Sound 🔊 1

Limit results: Any Audience ⬍ Any Content ⬍ Any Format ⬍ (Search)

◆ **City of dreadful delight : narratives of sexual danger in late-Victorian London /**
Author: Walkowitz, Judith R. Publication: Chicago : University of Chicago Press, 1992
Document: English : Book ⊕ Internet Resource
Libraries Worldwide: 616
More Like This: Search for versions with same title and author | Advanced options ...
⊙ See more details for locating this item

◆ **A prescription for murder : the Victorian serial killings of Dr. Thomas Neill Cream /**
Author: McLaren, Angus. Publication: Chicago : University of Chicago Press, 1993
Document: English : Book ⊕ Internet Resource
Libraries Worldwide: 606
More Like This: Search for versions with same title and author | Advanced options ...
⊙ See more details for locating this item

⊕ **A man's place masculinity and the middle-class home in Victorian England /**
http://www.netLibrary.com/urlapi.asp?action=summary&v=1&bookid=52847
Author: Tosh, John. Publication: New Haven [Conn.] : Yale University Press, 1999
Document: English : Internet Resource 🖳 Computer File
Libraries Worldwide: 490
More Like This: Search for versions with same title and author | Advanced options ...

Figure 2.1 Worldcat results for subject category 'Sex role – England – History – 19th century'

Online bookshops

Online bookshops provide powerful bibliographic searching tools as an inadvertent by-product of their efforts to sell books. Unlike library catalogues, they don't allow you to download references easily and often make it difficult to find the citation information you need. They make short descriptions of books available, often including a listing of contents, and allow us to search for books in novel ways. The online bookshops discussed below also provide significant added information on books.

Amazon.com/Amazon.co.uk/Amazon.ca Amazon has become an increasingly powerful and important source of bibliographic information over the past few years and provides several unique ways of locating books by subject. Through arrangements with a variety of other booksellers, including second-hand booksellers, it provides one of the largest bibliographic databases in existence.

'Customers who bought this item also bought' provides a unique insight into the books which other people interested in your subject area are currently buying, potentially flagging up recent publications which you weren't aware of. The option to 'Search for books by subject' presents a list of all the subject categories a book fits into. You can select some or all of these categories to get a list of very closely related books.

When you search Amazon by subject you will often be presented with a 'Listmania' column on the side, providing links to short lists of books compiled by people interested in the subject area. For academic topics, a substantial proportion of these are compiled by PhD students. They often provide a commentary on the books, and can sometimes serve as a useful guide to some of the current literature. When you select a list you will also get links to other Listmania lists on related subjects and you can also do a keyword search of all Listmania lists.

Amazon.com (but not Amazon.co.uk) presents you with lists of 'capitalized phrases' (CAPs) and 'statistically improbable phrases' (SIPs) which appear in each book. The SIPs are rare phrases, and many of them are likely to be uniquely associated with the subject you're interested in. They can be a useful source of very specific keywords for use in future searches. They are only provided for books with the 'Search inside this book' or 'Look inside this book' facility.

While reader reviews on Amazon are quite uneven in quality, reviews of academic books are often quite useful because people who have gone to the trouble of accessing the academic literature on the topic generally have more than a casual interest in the topic. In addition, Amazon often links to reviews in print publications.

Amazon.com includes citation searching features, providing links to books cited in the book you're looking at and 'Books that cite this book'. These features appear to be limited to citations in books on the Amazon database that have the 'Search inside this book' feature and therefore miss out on many citations.

The Amazon bookstores serving separate national markets have quite different collections of books and it is well worth searching Amazon UK, Amazon Canada and Amazon in the USA for English-language books. Amazon's 'Search inside this book' feature allows you to search the full text of selected books and is dealt with below along with other services providing access to the full text of books online.

Goodreads (**www.goodreads.com**) This is a kind of social network for book readers that also provides many of the features we find in Amazon. You can join and create groups and add 'friends'. The reader reviews and the 'listopia' lists can be useful research resources.

Blackwell's (**bookshop.blackwell.co.uk**) Includes reader reviews and ratings and a 'People who bought this also bought' heading. It provides library classification numbers.

Barnes and Noble (**www.bn.com**) This site provides short extracts from press reviews of books and allows you to search for 'more on this subject' by ticking the relevant subject classifications. They include a 'People who bought this book also bought' section.

Search tip

Tracing a book through its ISBN

Occasionally, you may need to gather as much information as possible on a particular book. Enter the book's 10 or 13 digit ISBN into Wikipedia's 'book sources' search (**en. wikipedia.org/wiki/Special:BookSources**). This retrieves links to the records for this book in numerous sources, including Amazon, Worldcat, Google Books and numerous library catalogues. It also provides links to related editions.

Full-text books online

In the past few years there has been a dramatic expansion in the availability of full-text books online, in a variety of different forms. While many of these texts, such as the reference books mentioned above, are bundled together into collections open to paying subscribers, many other texts are freely available online to varying degrees. In addition to the large commercial e-book market, and the significant number of free e-book titles available through online bookshops, the full text of books is made available online in a variety of other ways. Printed books originate as computer files these days and it is a relatively simple matter to make them available online whether or not they are sold as e-books. In addition, a number of projects have been systematically scanning in the text of older books. Once online, they can be searched much more quickly and flexibly than the printed version, and searched as part of a wider collection of books. The fact that we can now do keyword searches across millions of book titles is revolutionizing the way in which we use books. Now that it is an easy matter to identify the two or three paragraphs in a book that relate to our precise query, the temptation is strong to do no more than look at the few sentences of text that surround our query without engaging with the book as a whole, not that this is a big problem. There will be core texts that you need to read from cover to cover and others that are valuable to you only for a passing reference that they make to your topic.

Google Books (books.google.com)

Google Books has become a truly phenomenal resource over the past few years and now searches a database of over 7 million books. Initially, Google made arrangements with thousands of individual publishers to make the full text of their books searchable. This created a large searchable collection but it was far from comprehensive. Then Google embarked on their 'Library Project' in collaboration with a number of academic research libraries and public libraries to systematically scan in their entire collections of books in order to create something close to a complete and comprehensive repository of all the books ever published. Google has run into repeated legal difficulties as many publishers and authors of the books they were scanning contested their right to do this. Google argued that since they weren't providing users with access to the full text of these books, but only with the facility to search the full text, they weren't infringing copyright laws. In 2005 a coalition of authors and publishers brought Google to court claiming breach of copyright, bringing this Google project to a halt (BBC News, 2005; Wyatt, 2005). The dispute had still not been settled by 2011. If and when it is settled, Google has proposed providing free access at a limited number of computers in US public libraries and academic libraries while also selling access to the database on a subscription basis. If a book is out of copyright, you can view the full text. In the case of most books, you can view only a few sentences around your search term, or a limited number of pages, depending on the arrangements made with individual publishers. The advanced search allows you to search by author and title and to limit your search by date. You can export citation details for individual books.

Google Scholar (**scholar.google.com**) provides a significantly different way of searching the Google book collection, providing information which is unavailable through Google Books. A result in Google Scholar provides a 'Library search' link which will connect you to a Worldcat entry for the book and allow you to see if the book is held by a library near you. The title links you to the book in Google Books, if it is included there, and to publication details in **getcited.org**, if it is not. The 'cited by' link will bring up a list of sources in which the book is mentioned, including books, academic articles and a large number of pages from the open Web.

Search tip

Printing from Google Books and Amazon Books

You can download and print out-of-copyright books on Google Books but you cannot do this for the vast majority of titles that you find there, even though you will be able to see extracts on the screen in front of you. If you only want to print a few pages, you can get around this problem by taking a picture of your screen. On a PC, press the 'Print Screen' key on your keyboard, then paste into the image-editing program you usually use to view/edit pictures and crop it. Then print the image. On a Mac, use the 'Grab' utility to 'capture' the part of the screen that's relevant to you and save it as an image which you can then print.

Creating a personal library online

The newest research management tools allow us to build up comprehensive personal libraries of the articles we use, and allow us to search the full text of these personal libraries. It is much more difficult to do it for books, unless you purchase all of the books you want to use as e-books. Google Books' *My library* feature allows you to partially remedy this problem by adding books from Google Books to a personal library. To use the feature you need a (free) Google account. Once logged into Google Books through this account, you can create 'bookshelves' for your various research areas. Once you have built up your library you can run searches that are restricted to the books in your library. Although you can organize the books by topic in 'bookshelves', you cannot, unfortunately, limit your search to an individual bookshelf or a set of bookshelves. If Google were to add this feature, it would significantly increase the value of this resource. Every time you search Google Books the search results will indicate whether a book is already in your library or not, making it easier to fill the gaps in your collection through general searches on your topic. You can't be certain of course that you have done a comprehensive search of the full text of all of the books in your 'My library' given that Google Books does not search the full text of all of its titles, but coverage is strong and extensive enough to make it a valuable exercise nonetheless.

Google books

My library

My Google eBooks (3)	🔒
Purchased (0)	🔒
Reviewed (0)	🌐
Recently viewed (0)	🔒
Favorites (0)	🌐
Reading now (0)	🌐
To read (0)	🌐
Have read (0)	🌐

Create new bookshelf

Figure 2.2 My Library image

This kind of resource suggests new ways of searching that are significantly different from the techniques we use in most databases. You can't use broad search terms online because they bring up too many irrelevant results, but you can use them to great effect if you are searching a tightly bounded, personalized set of sources. If you remember an argument made in one of the books you read but can't remember which book, you can search for it using the kind of simple broad searches that are usually ineffective. If you remember only that the sentence you want to quote includes the word 'treachery', for example, a simple search on that word might be enough to locate it.

In a tightly bounded collection like this we can search for the name of an article or author to examine how a particular piece of work has been discussed in the literature. We can search on a broad concept such as 'genealogy' or 'hierarchy' to see how this concept has been discussed in our particular research area. It becomes much easier to identify how a particular metaphor or argument is deployed in your field. Your personal library has a URL which you can pass on to colleagues to allow them to search bookshelves that you choose to make 'public'. A research team can build a shared library of books.

Amazon's 'Look inside' (amazon.com, amazon.co.uk or amazon.ca)

This service is similar in many ways to Google Books. As well as selling e-books, Amazon has made arrangements with a large number of individual publishers to make the full text of their books searchable online. The arrangements made with individual publishers determine the level of access you can get to the text around your search terms. You can't view or print entire books, but in many cases you can read the full text of the page on which your search term appears. Where the full text is not searchable, 'Look inside' often allows you to view the index and contents pages and sections such as the bibliography. In some cases, **Amazon.co.uk** provides full-text searching of a book not available for full-text searching in **Amazon.com** and vice versa, emphasizing once again that it's often worth doing a search on both. In addition, all three of the Amazon services available in English can give radically different results for the same search on a specific phrase. A search that brings up 20 results in amazon.co.uk might bring up only one in amazon.com and results are laid out differently in each of the services. While coverage is uneven and far from comprehensive, it includes many of the largest and most important academic publishers, providing access to vast numbers of high-quality, recent academic books.

By allowing us to simultaneously search the full text of hundreds of thousands of books it provides a way for us to identify books which make reference to very specific issues we are interested in. It will turn up works that you would probably never find by any other route because the book as a whole does not relate to your subject area even though it may have a useful page or two directly relevant to your research topic. It is most appropriate for 'needle in the haystack' searches at the later stages of your research rather than for general subject searches. In searching the full text of bibliographies in books it also provides a new kind of citation search. Searching for the full title of a book in Amazon, and the author surname if necessary, will yield a list of references and citations in other books, providing another way to identify texts which refer to the key works you are interested in.

It can also be useful to carry out searches of individual books, in either Amazon or Google Books. With a copy of the book beside you, the 'Search inside the book' feature can supplement the index and contents page in the printed versions. Print indexes can sometimes be quite weak and the online search can be a valuable supplement when searching for an elusive reference in an individual book. The Amazon and Google full-text collections overlap but both services include the full text of books not available from the other.

Search strategy

Using a key text to identify related works

A good book on your topic can be the ideal starting point for identifying other high-quality work directly relevant to your research. It is certainly a much faster and efficient way to find related work than doing keyword searches on massive databases.

(Continued)

(Continued)

First, you need to identify a book that is central enough to your topic that many people writing on the topic feel they need to reference it. At the same time it needs to be specific enough that it is not cited by people from a wide range of disciplines.

For research on magic, demons and witchcraft in medieval Europe, for example, a good starting point might be a book such as *Europe's Inner Demons*, by Norman Cohn. While not everyone agrees with the conclusions of the author, it is a key text on the topic and a large proportion of people writing on this area are likely to reference it. At the same time your search will exclude the masses of popular literature on the topic which don't make reference to academic work like this.

This search does not need to be a marathon affair. Ten minutes should be all it takes to quickly search a service. There is no need to check out every vaguely promising looking item. If nothing looks useful at first glance simply move on quickly to another service. The basic principle is to do large numbers of quick searches using the same specific search term. No need to linger. In the example below, Amazon.com is used but the same general approach can be usefully applied to Amazon.co.uk, Google Scholar, Google Books and Worldcat.

After you have used a few services you are likely to find that your searches are yielding diminishing returns and I don't suggest you exhaustively mine all of these.

On the Amazon.com page for *Europe's Inner Demons,* the section on 'Customers who bought this item also bought' (see Figure 2.3 below) turns up several books which appear to be directly relevant. Following the link to one of them, *Witchcraft in Europe: 400–1700*, we see that this is a collection of primary sources on the topic. The fact that it comes from a university press provides another indication that it is an academic book, while reader reviews indicate its relevance to historical scholarship on 'witchcraft'.

The 'Look inside' link to the 'table of contents' for this book allows you to confirm its academic character and lists the chapters, giving you a better idea of whether some or all of them are directly relevant to your research. You can 'Search inside the book' to see if it contains information on very specific topics of interest to you.

The section for 'Customers who bought this item also bought' on this page points in turn to several more academic books which appear to be directly relevant to the topic and which can also be explored through Amazon.com.

There is a link here to a Listmania list on 'Great Witchcraft Books', which brings together about a dozen books, the bulk of which are academic. You begin to see that four or five of the books are mentioned again and again, providing a crude indication that they are regarded as key texts.

There is little need to use the more sophisticated searching options available here because the 'Customers' list has provided more than enough to start with. If it hadn't turned up anything, your next step would be to explore some of the other options on the page for *Europe's Inner Demons*, including 'Similar items by subject' and 'Citations', which lists books that cite this book as well as books that are cited in it.

The sponsored links on these pages are of no use, pointing as they do to a world of magic and witchcraft merchandising which bears little relation to academic study of the topic. This is also the case with some of the Listmania lists on the topic, which are dominated by popular books with little or no connection to the academic debates. They provide a hint of the vast store of popular materials on the subject that you have almost completely excluded from your search results simply by using a key academic text as the starting point for your search.

The result of this quick search is a list of eight to ten key academic books in the area which are directly related to your topic and whose contents you can explore if the 'Search inside the book' facility is available for those particular books. If it isn't, you can check **books.google.com** to see if they make the full text searchable. These books can in turn lead you to other books and to articles. When you come to search the databases of journals, which is dealt with in Chapter 3, you can search for articles which cite any of perhaps three or four of these key texts. You can also use them as search terms when you are looking for material on the open Web.

In the process of doing this search you will also have become familiar with some of the core terms which are used by all of these authors, but which relate uniquely to this subject area. These can also be a useful source of search terms when you continue on to do keyword searches of the full text of articles and the open Web.

Customers who bought this item also bought

The Pursuit of the Millennium : Revolutionary Millenarians and Mystical Anarchists of the Middle Ages (Galaxy Books) by *Norman Cohn*

Cosmos, Chaos, and the World to Come, 2nd Edition by *Norman Cohn*

The Night Battles : Witchcraft and Agrarian Cults in the Sixteenth and Seventeenth Century by *Carlo Ginzburg*

Witchcraft in Europe, 400-1700: A Documentary History (Middle Ages Series) by *Alan Charles Kors*

The Witch-Hunt in Early Modern Europe (2nd Edition) by *Brian Levack*

Explore similar items: in Books

Figure 2.3   Books bought by Amazon.com customers who bought *Europe's Inner Demons*

E-books

The spread of e-book readers in recent years has facilitated a shift by both publishers and booksellers from print to e-books. E-book readers such as the Kindle, the Nook and the Sony Reader allow you to search and annotate and highlight text from your collection of e-books but they have limitations as research tools. You have to purchase the books before you can search them (unless they are out of copyright) and they are not yet well integrated with referencing software. The main advantage of e-books is that they can be purchased and browsed and searched much more flexibly than printed books. Publishers are increasingly bundling related books into collections and selling access to the package as a whole. Users aren't expected to read cover to cover, but to download or print a chapter here and a page there. E-book software generally allows you to mark important passages and add your comments and sometimes allows you to copy and paste quotes into Word documents, automatically generating citations. Academic libraries are increasingly purchasing access to e-books instead of, or as well as, purchasing print titles, and you may find that much of your e-book usage takes place online, through your library's website.

Project Gutenberg (**www.gutenberg.org**) One of the earliest online book projects, this is dedicated to providing free access to books that are out of copyright and currently has a collection of over 36,000 free e-books.

The Internet Archive (**www.archive.org**) This includes the full text of around 3 million out-of-copyright books, including over a million books digitized in cooperation with libraries and foundations.

Taylor and Francis (**www.ebookstore.tandf.co.uk**) Several thousand of their printed books are available as e-books and there are a variety of ways to search and buy content from these books. Unlike many of the big online services, this service is aimed at individual users as well as institutions and is extremely flexible. The ePrint and eCopy options allow you to print and copy content for as little as a few pence or cents per page in some cases. eSubscribe allows you to buy access to material for as short a timespan as 24 hours. eCompile allows you to select content from a wide range of books, putting together a page here and a chapter there to create your own customized e-book. You can then annotate and bookmark items within the customized e-book. It's all very innovative, and has the potential to change the way we think of books as a research resource, from something you read to part of a collection you search. But all of these facilities are strictly limited in value because of the fact that they are limited to the output of one, albeit large, publisher.

When the various e-book services are fully standardized and integrated with research management packages it will become a far more attractive proposition to make intensive use of e-books.

Oxford Scholarship Online (**www.oxfordscholarship.com**) This service includes almost 5,000 academic books published by Oxford University Press and new titles are added regularly. All users can search and view book and chapter abstracts freely and these abstracts are now also searchable via Ingenta and Proquest, databases that used to be limited to academic articles. Since Ingenta is also searched by Google Scholar, you also search the Oxford Scholarship collection when you search in Google Scholar. This emphasizes the rapid multiplication of routes to any given document and the breakdown in the distinction between book chapters and journal articles. Subscribers, or those whose institutions are subscribed, can view the full text of books and download references.

Book reviews

Book reviews in journals, papers and magazines are now much more accessible and easy to search online. In addition, reader reviews posted to online book-shops and catalogues provide a valuable new resource, even if the quality of reviews is uneven. Some academic websites have used the Internet to distribute new kinds of book review. These are longer than normal because they don't suffer from restrictions on space, and often allow a right of reply to the reviewed author. These developments are radically altering the nature of book reviewing, by increasing the levels of debate and dialogue taking place around books.

Amazon.com/Amazon.co.uk customer reviews. The selection of reviews on these two services overlaps, but not completely.

Books in Print (**www.booksinprint.com**) This includes over half a million book reviews.

Book Review Index (**www.gale.com/BRIOnline**) This is a database of reviews of approximately 5.6 million items from thousands of journals, newspapers and magazines going back as far as 1969. It is available if your institution has subscribed.

H-Review (**www.h-net.org/reviews**) This is entirely devoted to distributing reviews of academic books in the humanities and the social sciences, and is freely accessible to all. The selection is quite limited but the quality is generally high.

Publishers

Publishers like to develop concentrated expertise in specific areas. When your research is at an advanced stage you will probably be able to identify a few publishers who specialize in your areas of interest. At this stage it can be useful to sign up to their alerting services. You can generally select the subject areas you are interested in and receive regular email alerts when new books in those areas are published. Below are a few examples of publisher alerting services:

- Wiley-Blackwell E-mail Alerts (**www.wiley.com/bw/ealerts/**)
- Cambridge Alerts (**www.cambridge.org/alerts**)
- Sage Product Alerts (**www.sagepub.com**)
- Taylor and Francis eUpdates (including Routledge) (**www.taylorandfrancis. com/resources/email_alerts**)
- University of California Press Enews (**www.ucpress.edu**)
- The University of Chicago Press New Releases Notification (**www.press.uchicago. edu/mailnotifier**)

Exercises

Exercise 1: Finding information about a book

Choose a key book related to your research topic and search for the book in at least three of the following services:

- Worldcat
- Amazon.com
- Amazon.co.uk
- Your library catalogue
- Google Books
- Google Scholar
- Books in Print

1 List the information about the book provided by each of these services (including reviews, facilities to access information on related books, and access to some or all of the book's content). You don't need to list all the citation details, just note whether they provide full citation details or whether certain citation elements are missing.
2 Which of these services allows you to download references?
3 Briefly outline the differences in the type of information provided on the book by the different services.
4 What was the most useful feature of each service?
5 Do any of these services provide useful information about the book that is not available in any of the other services?
6 Were any of the reader reviews useful? In what way?
7 Briefly describe the strengths and weaknesses of each service in providing information on your selected text.

Exercise 2: Finding a reading list

Use a search engine such as Google or Yahoo or one of the online teaching resources discussed in this chapter to identify a course syllabus that provides a reading list and/or topic summaries that are directly relevant to your research topic. Note that many syllabi do not include reading lists.

1 Write a paragraph describing how you found the relevant syllabus, noting in particular any difficulties in locating it.
2 Did you find that your topic was classified or described differently at different universities? Briefly describe any notable differences.

Exercise 3: Using a key text to identify related works

Choose a key book related to your research topic. In each of the services listed below, search for the book and then use all of the features that allow you to find related books to identify at least three other books directly relevant to your research.

- Amazon.com
- Amazon.co.uk
- Worldcat
- Your library catalogue
- Google Books
- Google Scholar

1 List the three books identified through each service.
2 Write a short comparison of the three services' usefulness for identifying related books.

Exercise 4: Finding books that cite a book

Identify a key book in your research area. Use the following services to identify other books that make reference to it.

- Amazon.co.uk
- Amazon.com
- Scholar.google.com
- Books.google.com

1 List the books you have identified through each service.
2 How much overlap is there between the results returned by the different services?
3 Is there any difference in the results returned by Amazon.com and Amazon.co.uk?
4 Discuss the strengths and weaknesses of each service.

Exercise 5: Finding book reviews

Identify a key book in your research area. Gather all of the reviews of the book that you can find online, using all of the following services. If your library is not subscribed to the two subscription services, just leave them out.

- Amazon.com
- Amazon.co.uk
- Books in Print (www.booksinprint.com)
- Book Review Index (www.gale.com/BRIOnline)
- H-Review (www.h-net.org/reviews)
- Google Scholar
- Google Books
- A general search engine such as Google or Yahoo

1 List the reviews, including the details of the publications they appeared in (if they were published).
2 Compare the relative usefulness of the various services in identifying useful reviews. Do some reviews appear in more than one source?

THREE

Articles

Understanding academic articles

The development of the Internet has made academic articles much more accessible to a wider audience. They have become a central resource for students at all levels, and there has been a sharp increase in the readership of journal articles. There are difficulties with this. Journals are meant to provide a forum for cutting-edge research and many academic articles are aimed at readers with extensive background knowledge in the relevant area. Academic articles often engage with a very specific aspect of a longstanding debate and readers are in danger of missing the point of the article entirely unless they have at least an outline understanding of the key debates in the area. This doesn't mean that you shouldn't use journal articles until you've mastered your field, but it does mean that you should make sure you understand the wider debates in which these articles are located. The references in journal articles, pointing to work which authors regard as the most important work on their topic, provide a powerful resource for identifying further key books and articles in the relevant area.

Academic journals, alongside academic books, are seen as the prime location for academic or 'scholarly' debate, optimistically characterized as a kind of ongoing collective conversation in the pursuit of knowledge. Academics write for these 'peer-reviewed' journals without getting paid and the main customers for these journals are university libraries. Articles published in academic journals are subject both to editorial input and to peer review, which involves articles being assessed by those considered to be expert in the field. This level of quality control, while often criticized and far from flawless, sharply distinguishes academic articles from other kinds of publication.

The tangled maze

Academic articles are extremely accessible online but you will still face stumbling blocks. You will find it much easier to deal with these obstacles if you develop an understanding of the way in which these materials are organized. The story of academic article databases began decades before the Internet, when database companies began to store the title pages of academic journals. They allowed people to search the titles of articles and sometimes to search short descriptive abstracts too. These databases are referred to as 'indexing and abstracting databases'. They don't include the full text of articles but they remain a key research resource.

Over the past ten years virtually all of the major academic journals have made the full text of their articles available to subscribers via online databases. Some of these databases are restricted to the output of a single publisher, or of a small collection of publishers, and they are organized very differently from the indexing and abstracting databases. The full-text databases overlap with, but don't replace, the indexing and abstracting databases. It is worth using both.

The content of a database is determined by a set of commercial agreements between journals, publishers and database companies with the result that the numerous databases are a tangled maze of competing and overlapping services. The resulting overlap ensures that a single article can be listed in more than 20 different databases. At the same time, the overlap is far from complete. All of the databases index material not indexed anywhere else and different databases can differ widely in their coverage of the same publication. One database may cover a journal from 2002 onwards while another covers it back to 1994. The CrossRef system established by academic publishers (**crossref.org**) has linked together many databases and it has recently become much easier to find an article you want without checking the individual databases. Google Scholar takes advantage of these thickening links between databases to allow users to search a large selection of full-text article databases simultaneously.

Technical information: understanding databases

All of the information relating to a single document (author, title, publication details, abstract and perhaps the full text) make up the 'record' for that document. Each of these items of information is a separate 'field' in that record. Every record in the database will contain those same fields. When a record is broken into fields like this, it makes it much easier to search. You can limit your search to the author fields of all records, for example. This is exactly what you are doing when you 'Search by author' on a library catalogue or article database. As a result of this, it is possible to do a far more precise and sophisticated search on a well-structured database than it is on one of the big Internet search engines.

The linking revolution

Just as the distinction between books, chapters, articles and pages is being blurred, so too is the distinction between the different kinds of database. Indexing databases used to be a source of frustration because they provided information about articles but not the full text. Library catalogues provided information about books but couldn't tell you if they were available online, and databases of full-text articles were frustrating because many of them were limited to the output of a single publisher, ensuring that you would have to search several of them if you wanted to search all of the full-text articles available online.

We are currently in the midst of a linking revolution that is moving faster than almost anyone can keep up with. Libraries, publishers and database companies have been operating in a state of constant flux over the past ten years, but recent developments have seen the emergence of some common standards which promise to bring an end to much of the chaos and confusion for everyone involved.

One result of this linking revolution is that the distinction between a database that provides full text, a database that simply stores titles and abstracts of articles, and a library that simply catalogues the details of the journals it is subscribed to, is collapsing. These three alternative routes to journal articles are being linked seamlessly together and the emerging standards are transforming the routes by which we can move from one database and from one print publication to another. The end result is that we can reach the full text of an article almost as quickly through a library catalogue or an indexing database as we can through a full-text database.

The key to this shift is OpenURL links. These links make it easy to flick from one document to another regardless of which database they're hosted in. OpenURL links in services such as Google Scholar take you directly to the item in question or to your own institution's records on this article or book, allowing you to easily access the online copies that your institution has access to. It renders irrelevant the distinction between a full-text database and an indexing database because both of them can now lead you quickly to the full text. OpenURL linking is being increasingly used within articles in full-text databases to provide links to cited references. This makes it a much simpler matter to chase up references and makes academic articles much more like web pages, providing lots of hyperlinks to the full text of related documents. One of the frustrations of OpenURL linking is that it often reveals that your own library does not provide access to the article in question because it does not have a subscription to the journal.

More recently, article databases have integrated their services with social media such as Facebook, Google Plus and Twitter, allowing you to easily post an article that you locate in a database to your Facebook or Google Plus account or to tweet it.

Annual reviews (arjournals.annualreviews.org)

The annual reviews deal with several social science disciplines, including anthropology, environment and resources, law and social science, political science, psychology, public health and sociology. Articles in the reviews survey academic work on a particular topic, reviewing the debates and discussing significant recent work on the topic. They are among the most widely read academic articles because they provide a guide to the existing literature. You can limit your search to one review or search them jointly. You can search the titles and keywords of review articles using broad search terms to see if an article has been devoted to your research area. You can also effectively search for an article by searching the full text for a reference to the subject matter or to a key text on the topic and the surname of a key writer in the area. For example, a search on **"sociology of food"** brings up a 2002 review article on 'The Anthropology of Food and Eating'. The reviews can provide a useful way to learn about current debate in your area of research but note that many articles are pitched at a high level, aimed at describing the state of play in the field to those with a good grounding in the topic. You can also search these reviews through Google Scholar.

Google Scholar (Scholar.google.com)

The popularity and simplicity of Google has ensured that Google Scholar has rapidly become one of the most popular ways to search for academic articles and books. This has provoked a backlash from some, who point out that it is far less comprehensive and less clearly structured than established academic databases. The critics are right. Google Scholar is severely flawed and doesn't stand up to comparison with the established academic databases (for example, see Jacsó, 2005, 2011). The enthusiastic adopters of Google Scholar are also right, however. It provides a fast, simple way to access the academic literature without learning about lots of different databases. It's on the open Web, it's easy to use and it's free, although more often than not it guides you to articles that are not freely available to the public. If you're simply looking for the full text of an article whose title and author you know, Google Scholar is unquestionably the best place to start your search. If you want to find an academic article on a very specific subject, Google Scholar is more useful than ordinary Google because it limits your search to academic materials. It has an advantage over the big abstracting and indexing databases in that it searches the full text of collections rather than just the abstracts and keywords.

Among the full-text collections and databases searched by Google Scholar are Taylor and Francis, CSA, JSTOR, Ingenta Connect and Project Muse, all of them described in more detail below. These full-text databases used to be regarded as part of the 'Invisible Web' or the 'Deep Web', because the content was inaccessible to search engines. Google Scholar doesn't search all of the full-text databases, however, and it doesn't allow the kind of sophisticated searching that is possible if you search the databases themselves directly. Google Scholar only seems to search a fraction of the materials on these sites (Jacsó, 2005). You will get more results if you search on the sites directly. Google Scholar also searches a variety of open access repositories (see below) and a range of other materials from the open Web that Google classifies as 'scholarly' or academic, including materials from academic publisher websites and university websites. As such it is far broader than the article databases. This is useful if your search isn't bringing back enough results, but not so useful if you're already bringing back too many. Google Scholar is best used in tandem with the indexing and abstracting databases and the full-text databases rather than as a substitute. The other databases are better organized, more tightly limited to academic articles and books, and can be searched in a more sophisticated way than Google Scholar. The 'Cited by' feature in Google Scholar, for example, is quite crude compared to the citation searches possible in ISI Web of Science and Scopus, although it has the advantage that it picks up many more citations than they do. You will miss a lot if you rely entirely on Google Scholar. To facilitate the downloading of references from Google Scholar, select 'Scholar preferences' and choose your preferred reference management package from the 'Bibliography Manager' section.

Each Google Scholar result includes a 'Cited by' link to documents that cite the article or book concerned. In the UK and Ireland, the 'BL Direct' link connects you to the British Library's ordering service, allowing you to buy a copy of the

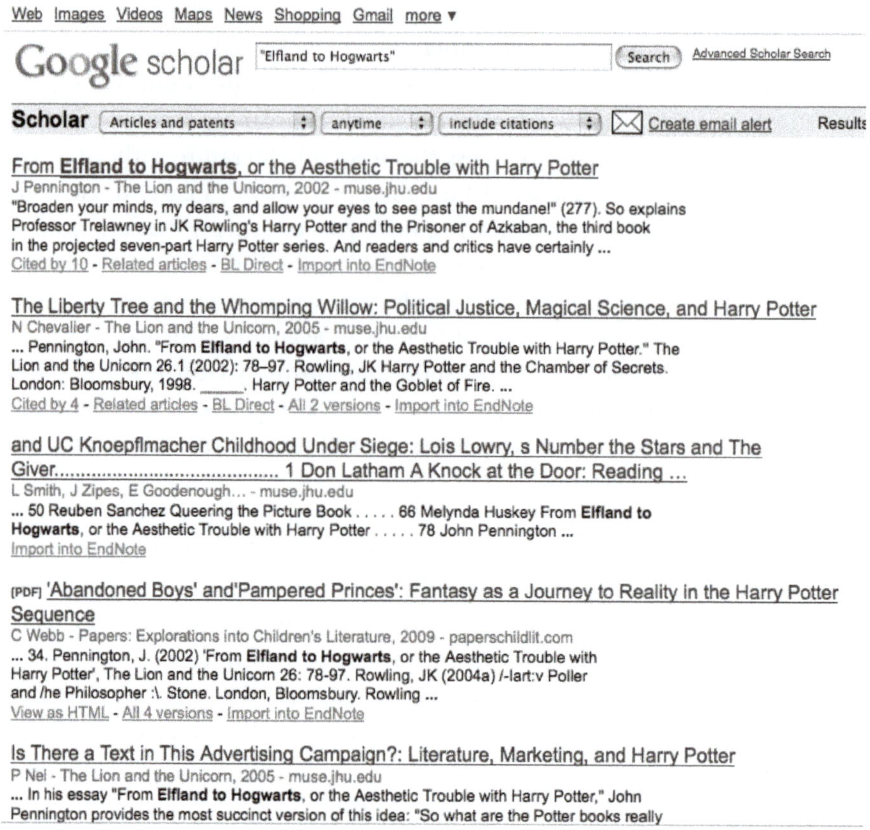

Google scholar "Elfland to Hogwarts" [Search] Advanced Scholar Search

Scholar (Articles and patents ◆) (anytime ◆) (include citations ◆) ☒ Create email alert Results

From **Elfland to Hogwarts**, or the Aesthetic Trouble with Harry Potter
J Pennington - The Lion and the Unicorn, 2002 - muse.jhu.edu
"Broaden your minds, my dears, and allow your eyes to see past the mundane!" (277). So explains
Professor Trelawney in JK Rowling's Harry Potter and the Prisoner of Azkaban, the third book
in the projected seven-part Harry Potter series. And readers and critics have certainly ...
Cited by 10 - Related articles - BL Direct - Import into EndNote

The Liberty Tree and the Whomping Willow: Political Justice, Magical Science, and Harry Potter
N Chevalier - The Lion and the Unicorn, 2005 - muse.jhu.edu
... Pennington, John. "From **Elfland to Hogwarts**, or the Aesthetic Trouble with Harry Potter." The
Lion and the Unicorn 26.1 (2002): 78–97. Rowling, JK Harry Potter and the Chamber of Secrets.
London: Bloomsbury, 1998. _____ . Harry Potter and the Goblet of Fire. ...
Cited by 4 - Related articles - BL Direct - All 2 versions - Import into EndNote

and UC Knoepflmacher Childhood Under Siege: Lois Lowry, s Number the Stars and The
Giver.. 1 Don Latham A Knock at the Door: Reading ...
L Smith, J Zipes, E Goodenough... - muse.jhu.edu
... 50 Reuben Sanchez Queering the Picture Book . . . . . 66 Melynda Huskey From **Elfland to
Hogwarts**, or the Aesthetic Trouble with Harry Potter . . . . . 78 John Pennington ...
Import into EndNote

[PDF] 'Abandoned Boys' and 'Pampered Princes': Fantasy as a Journey to Reality in the Harry Potter
Sequence
C Webb - Papers: Explorations into Children's Literature, 2009 - paperschildlit.com
... 34. Pennington, J. (2002) 'From **Elfland to Hogwarts**, or the Aesthetic Trouble with
Harry Potter', The Lion and the Unicorn 26: 78-97. Rowling, JK (2004a) /-lart:v Poller
and /he Philosopher :\. Stone. London, Bloomsbury. Rowling ...
View as HTML - All 4 versions - Import into EndNote

Is There a Text in This Advertising Campaign?: Literature, Marketing, and Harry Potter
P Nel - The Lion and the Unicorn, 2005 - muse.jhu.edu
... In his essay "From **Elfland to Hogwarts**, or the Aesthetic Trouble with Harry Potter," John
Pennington provides the most succinct version of this idea: "So what are the Potter books really

Figure 3.1 Google Scholar search results

article. If you have chosen a reference management package, there will be a link
allowing you to import the reference.

In many cases a result will provide a link to several versions of the article available online. Open access articles in particular can often be available in multiple versions at many locations.

Entries for books have a slightly different set of links. The 'More info @...' link will connect you to information about availability of the item via your own institution. The 'Library search' link will bring you to the Worldcat entry for the book, showing you a list of nearby libraries where the book is available.

Because there are now so many different routes to a single item, you may find that several of the links Google Scholar provides to an article all lead you to the same source. One of the biggest difficulties is the amount of redundant results it brings up, often returning multiple references to a single item (Jacsó, 2005). In the advanced search, you can restrict your search by subject area and date. You can also search on author, publication and title.

Accessing an article from a journal your institution is not subscribed to

You will often find that your institution is not subscribed to the online version of a journal in which you've located a vital article. In all likelihood you will have to order it by inter-library loan or pay a fee to get an electronic copy of the article, but it's worth trying a few other routes first.

1   Search Google Scholar on the title and author to see if this points you to a free copy of the article. Google Scholar points to multiple versions of the same article and will often turn up a version of an article that was originally delivered as a conference paper or published as a working paper and is freely available online. It may not be the exact same text but it will still be useful.
2   If the article is more than three years old and your institution is subscribed to JSTOR, search for it there. You may have access to back issues through JSTOR even if you can't access current issues and Google Scholar may have missed it.
3   Locate a home page for the author by searching for the name of the author and his or her university on a search engine such as Google, Yahoo or Bing. The author might provide a link to the full text of a version of this paper or to closely related work that might be equally useful.
4   Search an Open Access search engine such as *OAIster* (**oaister.worldcat.org**) to see if a version of the paper has been made freely available in an open access archive.
5   If it is an older issue of a journal, search your own library catalogue to see if the library has the print version of the journal.
6   If the journal is not included in any of the full-text databases, it may have a website through which it makes articles freely available on the open Web. This is particularly relevant for minor journals.

If you need to get a large number of articles from a journal your institution doesn't subscribe to, locate an article from the journal in OCLC ArticleFirst and select 'Libraries worldwide' to see if a nearby library holds the journal. If so, it might be worthwhile trying to arrange to get access to the journal there.

Indexing and abstracting databases

Indexing and abstracting databases provide citation details such as author, title, year and place of publication. They also include keywords (five or six words chosen by the author of an article to describe its subject area) and abstracts (short pieces of text describing the contents of an article). The indexing services originated with the first attempts to make information about articles available in searchable form, long before full-text availability online had been dreamt of. Because they are not concerned with whether a journal is available online in full text, they are much more comprehensive than the full-text services. They include articles from large numbers of journals that are not available in any of the full-text services. Users often found it frustrating in the past that these databases delivered information about articles but not the full text. OpenURL links now allow these databases to provide links to the full text of articles. In addition to that, some of these indexing services have begun to add large full-text collections, further breaking down the distinctions between these databases and the full-text databases.

A few big services attempt to be universal, to comprehensively cover all of the social sciences and humanities. The overlap in content between these services is huge but far from complete, and it is always worth trying a few of them. In most cases below, URLs are not provided because you will need to follow a link from your own library or university's website in order to gain access. All of these services allow you to download references.

OCLC ArticleFirst

This massive service indexes over 16,000 journals and other periodicals in the social sciences, humanities and popular culture, and includes over 27 million records. It includes current affairs magazines and reviews of books. Unlike many of the other databases listed here, it does not provide abstracts of articles and

Figure 3.2 OCLC ArticleFirst advanced search

therefore allows a much more limited search of the articles than is possible in those databases.

One of the weaknesses of OCLC ArticleFirst is the fact that it has no subject search and no option to search for articles related to the article you're looking at. You can browse or search their list of journal titles to see if they index the journals of most interest to you. You can limit your search to an individual journal. You can also limit your search to items which your library subscribes to and which you will therefore have access to, saving the frustration of turning up a large list of results which you can't access. Through an OpenURL link you can connect to your own library's records in relation to this article, which should link you directly to the full text of the article if your library has access to it. ArticleFirst provides the unique service of listing libraries that hold the journal in question.

ISI Web of Science (isiwebofknowledge.com)

ISI Web of Science, published by Thomson Reuters, includes the *Social Sciences Citation Index (SSCI)* and the *Arts and Humanities Citation Index (A&HCI)*. They can be searched separately or jointly.

It is the original academic citation database. It differs fundamentally from the other services listed above in that it deliberately excludes huge numbers of academic journals, setting a high threshold for inclusion in the database. This is intended to act as a quality control mechanism but it also serves to exclude many newer and smaller journals. In recent years more and more academic writers have taken to checking whether a journal is included in ISI before submitting to the journal. This is because citation information in ISI is used by many institutions as an indicator of the 'impact' of publications. If the journal you publish in is not included in ISI it will not show up in many of these bean-counting exercises. The result is that inclusion in ISI can have a huge impact on a journal's status and future. The core purpose of ISI Web of Science is to provide information on who is citing whom in order to provide a faster way of finding articles which are related to each other and to provide an indication of how much impact individual journal articles have. It provides a way to trace long-term academic debates through the references writers make to those who have gone before them.

It has great strengths and significant weaknesses. All of the information is organized in rigidly codified databases, giving it a strong organizational structure. As a result, you don't pick up the irrelevant material and duplicate results that Google Scholar generates, and you can carry out very precise searches. On the other hand, the same rigidity means that your search options are sometimes restricted too tightly. You can't search for an author's full name, for example, only by their surname and initials, and the database can't distinguish between authors with the same surname and initials. If the author you're searching for

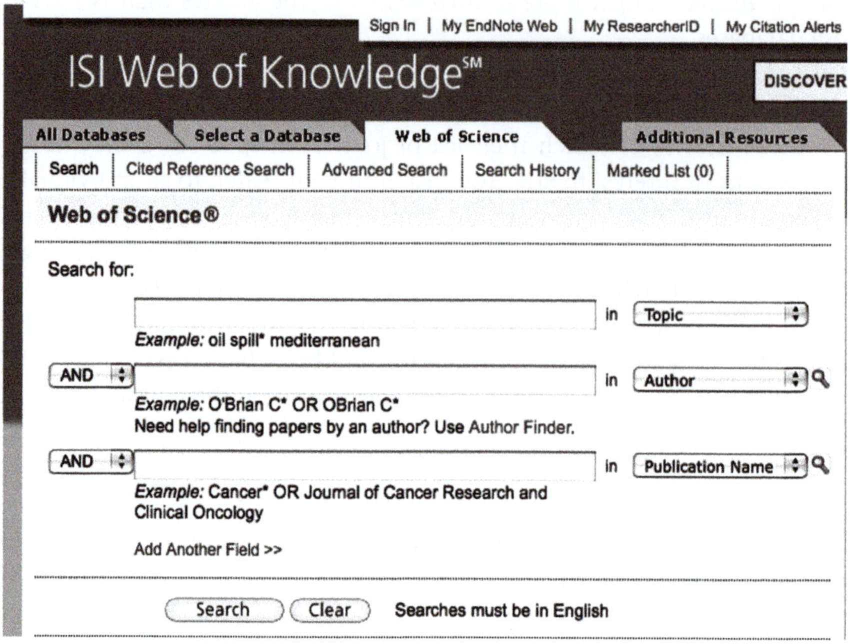

Figure 3.3 ISI Web of Science

has a common name, it can be difficult to get a full list of their publications. If you're searching for a publication title, you have to use the abbreviation ISI has assigned to it, leaving out common words like 'to' or 'the'. To do this often requires checking the 'Cited work index' to see how ISI has abbreviated the publication. If the item you are looking for is a book, you may well find that it has been abbreviated in two or three different ways and so pulling together a full list of articles that cite it requires you to look at all of these entries. It is not at all uncommon for an article to be listed more than once with slightly different details. Thus it is not uncommon for citations of a single article to be spread across two or more entries for the same article.

To bring back a list of articles that cite a particular article or book, do a 'Cited reference search' on the title and author. Click on the link to 'Times cited' to get a full list of all items which cite this article. You can then set up an alert to inform you when a new article also cites the same work. 'Find related records' brings back articles that cite any of the sources cited by the article you're looking at. This provides a powerful and novel way to identify clusters of related materials through shared references. ISI Web of Science also indexes book reviews, magazines and bibliographies, and allows you to restrict your search to a particular kind of item – to search only for bibliographies, for example. One major weakness of the service is the fact that it only deals with citations in articles and not in books.

Scopus

Established to rival ISI Web of Science as a major citation-based database, Scopus is far easier to use. It is possible that your institution will only be subscribed to one or the other, given the expense involved. It includes more than 5,000 journals in the social sciences and humanities and you can limit your search to these materials but it is not as strong in these areas as ISI Web of Science is. The record for every article includes hyperlinks to articles that cite it and to articles that it cites. Unlike ISI Web of Science, Scopus includes cited references from books. When you get a page of search results, you can refine your search, limiting it to certain publications, authors and types of document. You can set up search alerts and citation alerts. It has far shallower historical coverage than ISI Web of Science.

Other indexing and abstracting databases

Periodicals Index Online (**pio.chadwyck.co.uk**) This stands out for its historical depth, including items published three centuries ago and items in dozens of languages. It indexes over 15 million articles from more than 4,000 journals in the humanities and social sciences. It includes the full text of a few hundred journals.

CSA Illumina (**www.csa.com**) Illumina performs a joint search on over 100 abstracting databases and full-text databases maintained by CSA, including specialized databases devoted to a variety of social science subjects. These subject databases are dealt with below on an individual basis.

Academic Search Premier (EBSCO) (**www.ebscohost.com/academic/academic-search-premier**) This includes academic journals, newspapers and magazines, and includes the full text of over 4,600 journals across a wide range of disciplines. It allows you to limit your search to academic journals and to limit it to full-text sources.

The International Bibliography of the Social Sciences (IBSS) Focusing on anthropology, economics, politics and sociology, it indexes over 2,800 journals and around 7,000 books every year and is primarily aimed at UK universities. It has a strong focus on non-English language items that are neglected by many of the other databases. It indexes over 2.6 million items, including book reviews.

Ulrichsweb (**www.ulrichsweb.com**) This directory of periodical publications and academic journals provides information on a far wider range of publications than any of the other databases listed here and is an excellent source of information on rare and obscure sources. It lists the abstracting and indexing services that each individual journal is included in. It also lists all of the full-text databases through which each journal can be accessed and provides OpenURL links to many of the articles listed.

Zetoc (**zetoc.mimas.ac.uk**) This is the British Library's Electronic Table of Contents, a massive service indexing the contents of around 20,000 journals and 16,000 conference proceedings per year. It provides OpenURL links to the full text of articles, where available. It provides document delivery services to UK users. Like OCLC ArticleFirst, it indexes titles and keywords but not abstracts. British Library Direct (**direct.bl.uk**) is an electronic document delivery service that provides access for non-UK users to much of the material in the Zetoc database, a total of 9 million records.

The total number of articles or journals does not provide the best indicator of a service's usefulness. A geography database with 100,000 records may well contain far more that are of use to a geographer than a database with 20 million records covering everything from astrophysics to zoology. In Table 3.1 and the tables that follow, the figures given are minimum numbers. The numbers

Table 3.1   Indexing and abstracting databases

Database	Subjects	Journals	Total records	Other materials	Additional materials
OCLC ArticleFirst	Social sciences, humanities, popular culture	22,000+	27 million+	Current affairs magazines, reviews	Identifies libraries holding the journals
ISI Web of Science	Social sciences, humanities and science	23,000+		Reviews, magazines, bibliographies	'Cited reference search' and 'Find related records'
Scopus	All subjects	17,000+	44 million+	Conference proceedings, open access articles	Powerful reference linking
Periodicals Index Online	Humanities and social sciences	4,000+	15 million+		Deep historical coverage
CSA Illumina	All subjects				Joint search of over 100 CSA databases
Academic Search Premier	All subjects	4,000+ (full text)		Newspapers and magazines	
IBSS	Social sciences	2,800+	2.6 million+	Reviews 7,000+ books indexed every year	
Zetoc	All subjects	20,000+		16,000+ conference proceedings indexed per year	
Infotrieve	All subjects	54,000+	8.5 million+		

are constantly increasing. Different services estimate their total records and number of journals in very different ways and the figures listed here are not directly comparable. Nonetheless, they do give a crude indication of the relative size of these databases.

Search strategy

Searching for an article

In the example below you have the details of an article you are interested in. Ideally, you want to get the full text but if you can't get that, you want to get enough information to tell you if it is worth ordering or purchasing. In the course of this search you also want to explore information associated with the article, such as its references and the articles that cite it. For a research project on the academic debates around the Harry Potter novels, for example, you might be interested in an article such as: Pennington, John (2002) 'From Elfland to Hogwarts, or the Aesthetic Trouble with Harry Potter', *The Lion and the Unicorn*, 26 (1): 78–97.

Google Scholar: Because Google Scholar (**scholar.google.com**) searches so many full-text databases simultaneously, you are highly likely to find the article in Google Scholar and it is the best place to start. If you don't find it in Google Scholar, the next step would be to search one of the large indexing and abstracting databases such as OCLC ArticleFirst, ISI Web of Science or Scopus.

The title of this article is so distinctive that a short snatch of the title, such as 'Elfland to Hogwarts', brings back the Google Scholar entry for the article (see Figure 3.4). It also brings up several articles that cite it, some of them in the same journal, *The Lion and the Unicorn*.

If your library has access to the full text, there should be a link to the right of the entry. When you click on the link to the article it connects you to Project Muse, a full-text database that hosts *The Lion and the Unicorn*. If your library does not have a subscription, you are limited to viewing an excerpt from the text that gives a flavour of the contents.

The 'Cited by' link in Google Scholar brings up many of the articles already retrieved. The 'Related articles' link retrieves documents similar to the article. In the absence of a subscription to the journal, you can't get access via Google Scholar to the list of references cited by the article.

ISI Web of Science: In the 'General search' you can limit your search to the title of the article. In this example, the distinctive term 'Elfland' is enough to retrieve the short record for the article. If your library has enabled OpenURL linking, there will be an SFX or MetaLib or similar link here that will connect you to information about your library's holdings of online versions of this article. In my case, it shows that my library does not have the online version of the article.

(Continued)

(Continued)

Figure 3.4 Search results from Google Scholar

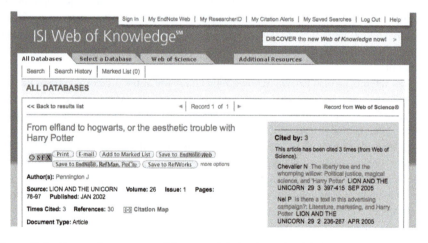

Figure 3.5 Extract from a record for an article in ISI Web of Science

The 'Times cited' link brings you to several articles that cite 'From Elfland to Hogwarts'. This includes some of the articles turned up by Google Scholar but it also turns up additional articles of interest.

In the short record for 'From Elfland to Hogwarts', click on the article title to get a fuller record (see Figure 3.5). In the fuller record you can click on the author name to get a list of publications by the author. This example demonstrates the limitations of ISI Web of Science. The author's name is reasonably common and this brings back a list of numerous articles on a wide range of topics by several different authors with the same surname and first initial. You can, however, create a set of results limited to this particular author if you then refine your query by category, subject area and author.

'View related records' searches for other articles that share at least one reference with 'Elfland to Hogwarts' but in this case the search is of little value. It brings up more than 600 results, none of which shares more than a few references with the article. Most of these refer to general texts on children's literature and there is nothing in the first page of results that seems to relate directly to Harry Potter.

The link to 'References' provides an abbreviated list of the books and articles cited in the article. Click on 'Find Related Records' to get the full details. You can set up a citation alert for the article here, something that is not possible via Google Scholar. Every time a new article that cites 'Elfland to Hogwarts' is included in ISI Web of Science you will get an email letting you know.

OCLC ArticleFirst: In ArticleFirst the single word 'Elfland' in the title search box is enough to bring back the record for the article. The record provides information unavailable through any other source, providing a list of 936 libraries worldwide that stock the journal. Surprisingly, my library is among them, even though the OpenURL link in ISI Web of Science led nowhere. Although my library doesn't have access to the online version, the print version is sitting on the library shelves. The search for the full text is over. Clearly, it was worth going beyond Google Scholar on this occasion. If the journal had not been available in my library, OCLC ArticleFirst would have shown me if it was available in a nearby library.

Scopus: 'Elfland' retrives the article, and a few others. You can click 'Citations' to view articles that cite this article but Scopus has not found any articles that cite this article because it has relatively weak coverage of the humanities.

Scopus indexes *The Lion and the Unicorn* back to 2002 (an indication of the relatively shallow historical range of this service) and you can click on the journal title to view tables of contents for every issue back to then, something it was not possible to do in ArticleFirst, ISI Web of Science or Google Scholar. You can quickly scan these contents pages to see if there are earlier relevant articles. Quick searches reveal that this journal is not available in Ingenta, HighWire or in JSTOR.

Although there was a lot of overlap between the four services dealt with above, each of them provided significant information unavailable in any of the other services. In addition to this, several of the major services did not cover this journal at all.

Specialized subject databases

The central feature that marks the specialized subject databases out from the big collections described above is exclusion. You can be sure that results will be tightly restricted to your subject area and closely related areas. If your research topic fits neatly within a single discipline, you may well find that it is much more fruitful to focus your searching on one of the databases below. You can do a quick mop-up search on the bigger databases later to make sure you haven't missed anything. Many of these specialized databases include abstracts written especially for these databases, covering not only articles but books too. In their concern to deal comprehensively with their particular subject area, they include relevant work from closely related disciplines and many of the smaller publications that are not indexed in any of the bigger databases. The list below includes many of the largest subject-specific abstracting and indexing databases in the social sciences and closely related disciplines in the humanities.

You can only get access to these databases if your institution is a subscriber, in which case there should be links from your library or institution's web pages. Several databases, including those hosted or run by CSA, now provide 'Cited Reference Linking' using OpenURL links to allow you to click directly from a cited reference to an abstract or the full text of the article cited. CSA also provide access to 'Scholar profiles' and 'Organization profiles', which provide information on researchers and research institutions.

Annual Bibliography of English Language and Literature (ABELL) Articles, books and reviews on English language and literature from 1920 onwards, and in any language. Subjects covered include drama, poetry, fiction, biography, literary theory and film. It can also be accessed via *Literature Online* (**lion.chadwyck. co.uk**)

Anthropology Plus (includes archaeology) Indexes articles, reports, commentaries and obituaries from several hundred journals and monographic series' from the nineteenth century onwards.

ASSIA: Applied Social Sciences Index and Abstracts (CSA) Dealing with social science and health, it contains over 375,000 records from more than 500 journals.

CIOS ComAbstracts (**www.cios.org/www/abstract.htm**) A database of article abstracts, books, bibliographic records and Internet materials on communication studies.

Columbia International Affairs Online (CIAO) (**www.ciaonet.org**) A major international affairs database which includes academic working papers, occasional papers from non-governmental organizations (NGOs), research reports, policy briefs, conference proceedings, books, journals and case studies written specifically for inclusion in CIAO.

Communication Abstracts (CSA) Covers communications and closely related areas, including abstracts of articles, reports, papers and books.

FIAF: International Film Archive Indexes film and television periodicals, and film archives.

Geobase A database of journals, books, conference proceedings and reports, covering both physical and social geography. It covers 2,000 journals and provides abstracts for over 600,000 items. You can limit searches by subject category.

Historical Abstracts Abstracts of articles, books, dissertations and smaller publications not included in the bigger databases.

International Political Science Abstracts (IPSA) Produced by the International Political Science Association. Articles in languages other than English are abstracted in French. All titles are translated into English.

Linguistics & Language Behavior Abstracts (LLBA) (CSA) Books, journal articles and dissertations on linguistics and related disciplines.

Modern Language Association Bibliography (MLAIB) (CSA) Articles, books, dissertations, bibliographies, proceedings and other materials from the 1920s onwards on literature, language, cultural studies, linguistics, folklore, film and theatre. It includes materials in more than 60 languages.

PAIS International: Public Affairs Information Service (CSA) This service indexes over 650,000 journal articles, books, government documents, statistical directories, grey literature, research reports, conference reports, publications of international agencies, microfiche and Internet material. It has a strong international emphasis, including publications from over 120 countries and a large collection of materials in languages other than English.

Philosopher's Index (CSA) Articles, books and book reviews on philosophy and closely related subjects, dating back to 1940.

Social Services Abstracts (CSA) Abstracts of journal articles from over 1,300 publications and abstracts of dissertations. It is focused on social work, human services and related areas, including social welfare, social policy and community development. It includes around 150,000 records.

Social Work Abstracts Produced by the US National Association of Social Workers, it includes over 45,000 records from more than 900 journals and dates back to 1977.

SocINDEX with Full Text (CSA) Abstracts for several hundred sociology journals and hundreds of related journals dating back to 1895. It also indexes books, conference papers, and a range of other sources. It contains full text for well over 300 journals, several hundred books and several thousand conference papers.

Worldwide Political Science Abstracts (CSA) Citations and abstracts in political science and related areas, including international relations, law, and public policy. It includes around half a million entries and indexes about 1,500 journals and other publications, with a heavy emphasis on material published outside the USA.

Table 3.2 Subject databases

Database	Subjects	Journals	Records
ABELL	English language and literature	–	860,000+
Anthropology Plus	Anthropology and archaeology	c. 900	800,000+
ASSIA	Social science and health	500+	375,000+
CIOS	Communication		50,000+
CIAO	International affairs	c. 60	
Communication Abstracts	Communication	160+	49,000+
FIAF	Film	300+	325,000+
Geobase	Physical and social geography	2,000+	600,000+
Historical Abstracts	History	2,100+	600,000+
International Political Science Abstracts	Political science	c. 900	
Linguistics & Language Behavior Abstracts	Linguistics	1,500+	360,000+
MLAIB	Literature, language, cultural studies, film and theatre	4,400+	1.7 million+
PAIS International	International public affairs	–	650,000+
Philosopher's Index	Philosophy	550+	320,000+
Social Services Abstracts	Social work, social welfare, social policy, community development	1,300+	150,000+
Social Work Abstracts	Social work and closely related topics	900+	45,000+
SocINDEX with Full Text	Sociology	Several hundred	1.6 million+
Worldwide Political Science Abstracts	Political science, international relations, public policy	1,500+	500,000+

Search strategy

Searching by author

Locate a home page for an author by searching for author name and university on Google, Yahoo or Bing. If somebody has written one good book or article in your area, the chances are that they have written other material that might be useful to you. If an author does provide a home page, it will often include some or all of the following:

- A more complete list of their publications than you are likely to get from any other source.
- Teaching syllabi and reading lists for their courses that may point you to other important sources in your area.
- Work in progress, which some authors make available online in order to advertize their work and to attract comments and suggestions.
- The full text of some of their articles.

Full-text articles online

Indexing and abstracting services can aspire to comprehensive coverage, or something close to it, because publishers are happy to have their articles indexed in all of these services, seeing it as a form of advertizing. Things are quite different when it comes to full text. Publishers make their money by selling the text. The full text of an article or chapter is generally hosted by one service only, while the citation details and abstracts may be available in 20 different databases. As a result, there is only a limited overlap between full-text databases. The collections below each represent only a piece of the full-text puzzle. You can search many of these services via Google Scholar but it's sometimes worth searching the full-text databases directly as well because they provide more powerful searching options.

HighWire (**highwire.stanford.edu**) This is a non-profit full-text database that aims to make academic literature more widely available. More than 2 million of the 6.7 million academic articles hosted here are available free of charge to anyone and HighWire is said to host the largest collection of free academic articles available online. In addition, HighWire hosts the full-text collections of a number of major publishers, including Sage and Oxford University Press, adding up to a total of more than 1,500 journals. Like all full-text collections, it is far from comprehensive, but as a collaborative project driven by academic as well as commercial concerns, it has very wide coverage and is particularly strong in the sciences where it hosts a large proportion of the most highly-regarded journals.

One of the strongest features of HighWire is its links to other full-text services and to indexing and abstracting databases. You can link directly from HighWire to the full text of cited articles held in other databases and to information on articles that cite the article you're looking at in ISI Web of Science and in Scopus, even if your institution does not subscribe to these. It also provides links to the related entry in Google Scholar and to the citation search in Google.

You can limit your search to reviews. You can set up alerts to notify you when a particular article is cited, or when an item matching your search terms is added to the service. You can also sign up for contents alerting for journals included in HighWire, avoiding the need to sign up separately with several different publishers. An innovative feature called 'My Favorites' allows you to limit your search to selected journals, allowing you to create a kind of personal search library.

Wiley Online Library (**onlinelibrary.wiley.com**) provides several advanced features that link it to the services of a range of other publishers and article databases. It includes over 4 million articles from more than 1,500 journals as well as reference books and almost 10,000 online books.

If your library subscribes to a journal, you can follow links to 'Citing articles' that cite the item you are looking at. You can view the list of references for an article.

These references may include OpenURL links to your own library's holdings of the material in question. You can sign up to receive an alert whenever a particular article is cited.

Ingenta Connect (**www.ingentaconnect.com**) hosts full-text journals from a variety of academic publishers. It includes over 15,000 publications and 5 million articles and also searches abstracts of book chapters. You can search titles, abstracts and keywords but not the full text of articles. To search the full text you can use Google Scholar, although apparently they don't cover all of the articles held in Ingenta. You can only access the full text of an article if your library is a subscriber.

JSTOR (**www.jstor.org**) JSTOR is concerned to archive older issues of journals. As a result it has much greater historical depth than most full-text collections, going back to the late 1800s, when most full-text collections barely go back to the early 1990s. The collection includes important key journals in the social sciences and humanities under arrangements that specify a 'moving-wall' of three to five years. That is, publishers allow JSTOR to put articles online three to five years after they are published. You will often find that you have access to older articles in JSTOR from journals whose current contents you can't access. You can only get access if your library or institution has subscribed to JSTOR.

Search strategy

Keeping up with new articles

After you have mined the big databases you need an efficient way to keep up with the vast quantities of new material that are added regularly.

1. Content alerts

Set up content alerts for the three or four key journals in your area and perhaps a few others in related areas. Every time a new issue is published you will get an email listing the contents. You can set up these alerts through HighWire (**highwire.stanford.edu**), *Wiley Online Library* (**onlinelibrary.wiley.com**), through the publishers (see below), or through the journal websites (search for the journal title in Google, Yahoo or Bing). Perhaps the quickest and most efficient way to set up alerts for multiple journals is to visit the websites of several major journal publishers where you can browse journals by subject category and simultaneously set up alerts for several journals with one or two clicks.

2. Search alerts

In the course of your searching you will develop a few search queries that work particularly well. You can sign up in many services for search alerts that send you an email each time a new entry matching your search query is added.

---

3. Citation alerts

If you find that citations of a key article or book produce a lot of useful leads, you can set up citation alerts to alert you when a new article cites this book or article. In many cases citation alerts can now be imported directly into reference management software.

Increasingly all of these alerting services are also available as RSS Feeds but email alerts are perfectly adequate.

Publishers

Some of the biggest academic publishers are responsible for thousands of journals and several of the big publishers maintain control of the full text of their journals online, marketing and presenting them as discrete research collections. Some of these collections are massive and include many of the most prestigious journals, but they are still limited to the output of a single publisher. There are now multiple routes to the articles the publishers provide online. You can get to most of them from the big indexing services and from Google Scholar, but you can often wring more out of the publisher sites by searching them individually.

You can search by author, title or abstract, search the full text of articles and download references in virtually all of the services listed below. Tables of contents and abstracts are usually freely accessible but access to the full text of journals is only available if your institution subscribes to the journal in question. Publishers generally have a more complete list of the contents of back issues of journals than do the big services such as Scopus and ISI Web of Science and are probably the best sites on which to browse back through the contents pages to get a sense of a journal's coverage over the years. You may sometimes find it useful to do a search limited to the full text of articles in one particular journal. This allows you to use broader search terms because you are searching such a limited selection of materials.

The services below also offer a variety of advanced search options, including the option to restrict your search to certain subject areas or to limit it to your personal selection of journals. In some of the services you can limit your search to reviews or to certain types of article. Most of them also provide alerting services. Increasingly, these services provide extensive links to related materials. Oxford Journals, for example, provides links to related content and citing articles in Google Scholar and ISI Web of Science. Many of these services allow you to save lists of articles but it hardly seems worth your while to do this with individual publishers when you can do the same for lots of publishers at once through large services such as Scopus or ISI Web of Knowledge.

- *Cambridge Journals Online* (**journals.cambridge.org**).
- *Elsevier Science Direct* (**www.sciencedirect.com**). One of the largest publishers of journals, but only a fraction of their journals are in the social sciences or humanities.
- *Oxford Journals Online* (**www.oxfordjournals.org**) Also available through HighWire.
- *Project Muse* (**www.muse.jhu.edu**) Over 400 humanities and social sciences journals published by JHU Press and a number of other university presses.
- *Sage Journals Online* (**www.sagepub.com**) Also available through HighWire.
- *SpringerLink* (**www.SpringerLink.com**) A massive collection but humanities and social sciences form only a small part of it.
- *Taylor and Francis Online* (**www.tandfonline.com**).

Figure 3.6 Sage Journals Online

Open access

The Internet is widely regarded as providing a unique historical opportunity for researchers to publish their own work online at little cost, bypassing the publishers. This dream of free circulation of academic work has not materialized. The publishers provide not only publication, but publicity, distribution and, above all, prestige, and it still makes sense for researchers to try to get published in the print journals. Nonetheless, there is an ongoing struggle to make academic work more widely available and increasing numbers of high-quality academic articles are now freely available online.

Table 3.3 Full-text databases

Database	Coverage	Journals	Total records	Full-text search
Google Scholar	All subjects, wide range of academic publishers			Yes
Wiley Online Library	Wiley-Blackwell Journals, all subjects	1,500+	4 million+	Yes
Ingenta Connect	All subjects, wide range of academic publishers	15,000+	5 million+	No
JSTOR	All subjects, wide range of academic publishers	1,000+	3 million+	Yes
Cambridge Journals Online	Cambridge Journals	250+		Yes
Elsevier Science Direct	Elsevier Journals	2,500+	10 million+	Yes
HighWire	All subjects, wide range of publishers	1,500+	6.7 million+	Yes
Oxford Journals Online	Oxford Journals (hosted by HighWire)	230+		Yes
Project Muse	Humanities and social sciences from several university presses	400+		Yes
Sage Journals Online	Sage Journals (hosted by HighWire)	630+	57,000+	Yes
SpringerLink	Springer Journals, and those of several other publishers	2,600+	5 million+	Yes
Taylor and Francis Online	Taylor and Francis Group Journals, including Routledge, Psychology Press and others	1,000+		Yes

Contrary to expectations that the Internet would make academic journals cheaper, academic publishers are charging the same or even higher fees for access to journals online. In response to this, the open access movement has developed tools to allow academics to self-archive their published articles, either in 'institutional repositories' at their own universities or in subject-specific archives, making them freely available. Research funding agencies, governments and universities are beginning to wield their considerable financial power to pressurize academics to make their research more freely available through such repositories. In the face of evidence that open access articles are cited more frequently than those in pay databases (for example, see Antelman, 2004), even some publishers are beginning to think about moving in this direction. Some journal publishers have begun to publish open access articles on the basis that the authors pay the costs of publication. Bizarre as it may sound, this is attractive to researchers in the many fields where research is primarily funded by grants. Researchers simply build open access publication costs into their research grants. This does not apply, however, to much research in the social sciences and humanities. The open access movement is committed to high academic standards, with repositories generally limiting their collections to materials that have been through some kind of academic peer-review process.

The terms 'escholarship' and 'eprints' are used to refer to academic work made freely available online. 'Preprints' are earlier versions of articles, usually slightly different from the final published version, while 'postprints' are the final version, after all the recommended changes have been made. It is easier for academics to make preprints freely available and one difficulty with the repositories is that they are heavy with preprints, working papers, conference papers and other work that has not taken a final definitive form. You have to make it clear in your own work that you are referring to such materials rather than to published articles. You may find that ultimately you need to get the final published version but at least the preprints allow you to decide how useful an article is to you. Open access repositories are searched by Google Scholar and are now included in several of the other indexing and full-text databases discussed above. This marks a recognition that they have become a major new source of academic literature beyond the published journals.

One of the main projects promoting the free circulation of academic publications is *HighWire* (**www.highwire.org**, see above). Although HighWire also includes subscription journals, it makes it easier for open access journals to operate by providing an infrastructure for hosting the journals.

OAIster (**oaister.worldcat.org**) is a search engine which allows you to do a joint search of over 1,100 open access repositories. In 2011 it included more than 23 million records. It includes the full text of books in some cases and the full text of many PhD theses and dissertations. It also includes a wide variety of materials, including images that you will not find in most academic databases. It is an excellent source to search if you want to check if you have overlooked obscure items related to your research. It also searches major academic resources on the open Web through its inclusion of materials catalogued by services such as Humbul, the UK catalogue of online academic resources in the humanities. OAIster records are also searchable through Worldcat.org.

Directory of Open Access Journals (**www.doaj.org**) is a directory of more than 2,000 free, full-text academic journals. You can do full-text searches of articles from around 500 of the journals.

Institutional repositories

Repositories vary in their criteria for inclusion. Some are more tightly restricted than others, but materials have generally gone through an academic quality control procedure of some kind. Below are two well-known examples of open access repositories. These and others are searched by OAIster.

Open Research Online (**libeprints.open.ac.uk**) The repository of the UK's Open University, it hosts research that has been authored or co-authored by members of staff. It only includes 'postprints', items which have been peer-reviewed or have gone through a similar process and which include the final changes made after review. It includes journal articles, book chapters and conference papers.

eScholarship, University of California (**escholarship.org**) One of the earliest repositories, it includes over 40,000 items.

Other article databases

The databases dealt with below include collections of academic articles but they are dominated by news and current affairs sources. They are not targeted as directly at academic users as the services dealt with above. Once again, the amount of overlap between each of these services is huge, while they also overlap substantially with many of the academic databases.

LexisNexis () Before the public had ever heard of the Internet, lawyers and the business community were using powerful online databases such as LexisNexis that provided the full text of articles from a vast number of sources. These databases were so expensive and so complex to use that companies hired specialized searchers just to search them. The full text of articles is often available in LexisNexis within hours of their publication and the service allows very sophisticated searching. Articles are split into separate fields that can be searched separately. In recent years LexisNexis has expanded and developed services aimed at university students and researchers. The legacy of catering to highly trained and highly paid professional researchers is visible in the rather sparse instructions for use. LexisNexis is not concerned primarily with citation details but with providing fully searchable full-text articles. It covers thousands of newspapers and academic journals in addition to a wide range of specialized materials such as news broadcast transcripts that are extremely difficult to get hold of by any other means. It bundles its services to target academic users with packages such as LexisNexis Academic and LexisNexis Professional.

In LexisNexis Professional you can restrict searches to publications from particular countries or to individual publications. A 'source directory' lists the different publications available to you. Including as it does vast numbers of newspaper stories, LexisNexis will generally return lots of results on all but the most specific queries. It is a good place to conduct very specialized searches using very specific phrases uniquely associated with your topic. Given the fact that the system baulks if you return over 1,000 results, it's a good idea to limit your search by date, restricting it to a few years. Unlike many of the other commercial services that focus on newspaper and magazine articles, LexisNexis allows you to download references.

Highbeam Research (**www.highbeam.com**) Unlike most of the services dealt with above, Highbeam has flexible pricing options aimed at users outside a university environment, allowing you to subscribe for a month. It is far less powerful than the databases covered above, but can be useful if you don't have access to those, and also as part of a 'needle in the haystack' search to make sure you haven't missed anything. It covers more than 6,500 newspapers, magazines, journals and other publications, and includes some key publications as well as a lot of marginal and specialized publications. It is very strong on news and current affairs sources.

Theses and dissertations

Many high-quality theses and dissertations are never published despite the fact that they contain valuable material of use to other researchers. There are a few online services now devoted to providing not only bibliographic detail about theses and dissertations, but to making the full text available, sometimes for a fee. In addition, the full text of many theses and dissertations is now freely available through open access repositories, which are searchable through *OAIster* (**oaister.worldcat.org**), discussed above. If you are doing an extensive piece of research, it is almost certain that there will be a few theses or dissertations of use to you, which contain valuable material not available elsewhere. You can also limit a search in WorldCat (**worldcat.org**) to theses and dissertations. The option appears on the search results page after you have done an initial search.

ProQuest Dissertations & Theses (**proquest.umi.com/login**) A searchable database of abstracts, keywords chosen by the authors and basic citation information such as title, date of submission and author. Coverage is not very deep in historical terms, going only as far back as the 1980s and 1990s in the case of many universities covered. Theses and dissertations completed since 1997 are available as pdf files, with a preview of the first 20 or so pages freely available to users at institutions that are subscribed. The full text of these theses and dissertations is instantly downloadable for a fee. The database is limited to items from universities that have arrangements with the database company. While virtually all North American universities are included, coverage is much patchier elsewhere in the world and is far from comprehensive.

Index to Theses (**www.theses.com**) A database of abstracts and citation details of more than half a million masters and doctoral theses accepted by universities in Great Britain and Ireland from 1716 onwards. The full text of more than 50,000 of these is available. Thus it has deeper historical coverage than dissertation abstracts while covering only the UK and Ireland. As a result, it contains much material not found in any other database.

EThOS: Electronic Theses Online Service (**ethos.bl.uk/Home.do**) A service of the British Library which allows you to search over 250,000 theses from more than 100 UK universities and research institutes, drawing on the digital repositories of these institutions. In many cases the full text is available for free and in many other cases you can order a copy for a fee.

Networked Digital Library of Theses and Dissertations (**www.ndltd.org**) This service contains more than 1 million records of electronic theses and dissertations, drawing on collections archived online at universities and a few larger commercial services. It provides the full text of dissertations, downloadable as pdf documents, often free of charge.

Dissertation.com (**www.dissertation.com**) This commercial service provides the full text of dissertations via the Internet, for a fee. You can search for dissertations by keyword or browse through lists of dissertations grouped by subject. There is a very limited selection.

Exercises

Exercise 1: Finding an article

Identify a key article on your topic. Search for the article using all of the following services that you have access to:

- OCLC ArticleFirst
- ISI Web of Science and/or Scopus
- Swetsnet
- Google Scholar
- HighWire Press
- Ingenta
- The journal publisher's full-text service (where one exists)
- A specialized subject database
- LexisNexis

In the case of each service answer the following questions:

1 Does it include the article you're searching for? If so:
2 Does it provide a link to the full text?
3 What other links does it provide in relation to the article?
4 How useful are these links?
5 What additional information does it provide about the article?

6 Can you download references?
7 What is the best feature of this service?
8 What are the weaknesses of this service?
9 Describe the extent of the overlap between the various services. If you could only use one source, which would you use and why?

Exercise 2: Searching by author

Locate a home page for the author of a useful article or book on your topic by searching for author name and university on Google, Yahoo, or Bing. Add the title of one of the author's publications to the search terms if necessary. Try to choose an author with several publications in your area. Note that many authors will not make any information available online. If you can't find a home page for one author, just keep trying different authors until you find a home page.

Look on the author's home page for lists of the author's publications, teaching syllabi, reading lists and the full text of their publications, where available. If the home page contains little information, search their university's site to see if information on the author's courses or their research record is available elsewhere on the site.

1 Describe any difficulties you had in finding an author's home page.
2 Describe the information you found.
3 For the same author, search for all articles by the author in:

   o OCLC First Search
   o ISI Web of Science and/or Scopus
   o Google Scholar

4 Compare and contrast the search results from these three services with each other and with the results from the author's home page. How much overlap is there?
5 Which of these sources provided the most comprehensive results?

Exercise 3: Setting up alerts

Identify two key journals in your area.

1 Set up content alerts for these journals. Briefly describe any difficulties in setting up the alerts.
2 Set up a search alert for a specialized search query that has already returned useful results for you from the article databases. Briefly describe any difficulties in setting up the alert.

3 Set up a citation alert for a key article or book in your area. Briefly describe any difficulties in setting up the alert.

Exercise 4: Searching by citation

Select one key article and one key book relevant to your research. The aim of your search is to find books and articles that cite them, on the assumption that some of them will be directly relevant to your research. If your selected book or article does not turn up any references, try another book or article.

a) Search Google Scholar using the title and author name

1 Follow the 'Cited by' links for all versions of the article or book returned in the results page.
2 List all of the unique sources that cite your book or article.
3 How many of the sources that cite your article or book are themselves academic books and articles?
4 How much duplication is there in the Google results?

b) Search ISI Web of Science (a 'cited reference search') or Scopus using the title and author surname

In ISI Web of Science you will often need to abbreviate titles, leaving out common words such as 'the', 'to', 'from', 'and'. If you can't guess the abbreviation, you'll have to go to the 'Cited work index' to see how they have abbreviated the item you're looking for.

List all of the unique sources that cite your book or article. Select one that seems relevant to your research and then click on 'Find related records'. List the first ten sources that this turns up.

1 How relevant are these results?
2 Which of the two services was more difficult to use? Why?
3 Which of the services turned up the most useful sources?
4 How much overlap is there between the sources they turned up?
5 What are the drawbacks of each of these services?
6 If you had to choose just one service to do a citation search on, which would you choose and why?
7 Is it worth searching both of the services you searched or is the overlap too large to make it worthwhile?

Exercise 5: Searching for a needle in a haystack

Choose a phrase uniquely associated with a specialized aspect of your topic. Search for the exact phrase in the following services. If the phrase is bringing back too many irrelevant results, choose a different phrase or refine the search by adding another term uniquely associated with your topic. If it brings back no results, choose another term.

Search at least five of the services listed below:

- Amazon.com
- Amazon.co.uk
- Google Book Search
- Google Scholar
- Ingenta
- Highbeam
- LexisNexis

In relation to each service you use:

1 List the useful results.
2 Discuss the extent of the overlap between the results retrieved by the different services.

FOUR

Subject guides

Searching the open Web

The previous two chapters on books and articles focused on highly structured databases. These databases are generally carefully managed and organized and are updated systematically. Authorship, context and responsibility are clear and unequivocal. This chapter and the following chapter deal with the open Web, online resources that lie beyond those databases. These resources are much less clearly organized, structured and bounded. Their authority and authorship are often unclear and their organizing principles sometimes impenetrable. They require different kinds of research approaches and skills.

Whatever subject area you are interested in there is a strong chance that someone has produced a guide to online resources on the topic. A good guide provides a useful way to identify the central online resources in your area. When you start devising queries for the big keyword search engines, you can concentrate on mopping up things that were missed by the guides. These guides vary in quality. The best of them amount to advanced annotated bibliographies, introducing you to resources in a very specific area. The worst of them are so broad and unfocused as to be useless. These guides are also referred to as indexes, catalogues, directories, gateways and clearing houses. One useful supplement to these guides is the large collection of one-hour tutorials on using the Internet in your research provided by a UK academic initiative, *The Virtual Training Suite* (**www.vtstutorials.co.uk**). Tutorials are targeted at individual subject areas.

Making sense of the chaos

Before exploring the guides it is useful to understand how things are organized on the open Web. There is a deep-seated reason for the disorganization on the open Web. There is a lack of agreed universal standards for the core elements that a web document should include. Email messages may seem as difficult to order and categorize as web pages but in email the software forces the key identifying marks of sender, recipient address and date on to every email. All of these can be used to set items in their proper context, as part of a particular discussion at a particular time. Web documents, by contrast, share only one universal identifying mark, their URL, the Uniform Resource Locator, which usually starts with **http://** and which is also referred to as the web address or the Internet address. Even this can shift and change. If the person in charge of a particular web document decides to rename the document or to move it around on his or her own computer, the URL changes. To compound the problem, the contents of web documents change, unlike printed matter and email messages. The same document at the same URL with the same title and author can have very different contents depending on when you look at it.

Sometimes it can take some serious detective work to even identify the author of a document. Finding out when it was written is often impossible and identifying the wider site or collection it is part of can require a fairly advanced understanding of the different ways in which websites are organized. Even major organizations often neglect to clearly stamp their authority on the documents they put on the web. You will often read about the lack of central authority and control on the Net, but it is this lack of agreed standards at a fundamental level which is perhaps the most deeply rooted source of the chaos. Having said all this, the bulk of well-established organizational websites, be they universities, governments, political parties, businesses or others, organize their sites clearly and coherently. The web may be a swirling mess and you may reach such sites by a circuitous route, but once you are there you will generally find that documents are well organized, and they will all have key identifying marks like author and date. While such sites are well structured, they are often structured very differently from one another.

Memory, forgetting and Internet archives

Huge volumes of material disappear from the Internet every day as the people running websites update their materials or allow their sites to become defunct. A webmaster who drags a document from his or her website to the trash may well be destroying the only copy of that information in existence anywhere. Even if a webmaster wants to preserve older versions of documents, there are no well-established and widely used standards for archiving out-of-date web documents. As a consequence, those archives of web documents that do exist vary greatly in their organization and structure. The result of this lack of concern for memory and archiving is that a huge volume of information is wiped off the Net every day and disappears entirely from the historical record. Materials that were online only a few years ago might as well never have existed. One major project, *The Internet Archive* (**www.archive.org**) (see Figure 4.1), is attempting to ensure that these materials are saved, but inevitably they are unable to archive everything. Sometimes they archive only a few sample pages from a site and they often miss out on other features of websites that are difficult to archive.

When the Internet Archive was first established it seemed an eccentric kind of venture. Few people saw the point of saving copies of websites that everyone already had access to. Just a few years on we are already beginning to appreciate just how important it is. Millions of sites have vanished over the past few years and millions of others have changed beyond recognition. The Internet Archive provides the only means of knowing that most of these sites ever existed. The Archive saves websites at regular intervals, every few weeks or months. When you go to the Archive you can explore how a website looked at various intervals during its history. If you are carrying out research on an organization of any kind, you may well find yourself using the Internet Archive to track the changes in the way that organization has represented itself online. These changes can be very revealing. Organizations often remove materials because they change their policies or because they realize that the materials show them in a bad light. To see the archives for an individual website or web page, type the URL into the Internet Archive's *Wayback Machine*.

The Archive has worked in partnership to develop a number of specialized collections. One of the best known of these is the *September 11 Web Archive* (**september11.archive.org**), a collection of more than 30,000 websites about the September 11 attacks that appeared in the three months after the attacks.

The Archive faces one major difficulty. The owners of domain names can block the Archive from making materials from that domain available to the public. This fact has punched huge holes in the Archive and means that organizations have the right to cover their tracks, to effectively destroy the previous records of materials they made available publicly. It also means that someone can buy the domain name of a defunct organization and then block public access to the archives of an organization they have nothing to do with.

The European Archive (**www.europarchive.org/**) is also dedicated to archiving online resources that might otherwise be lost, focused on Europe. It also aims to digitize important collections and make them freely available through partnerships with libraries, museums and other bodies and through creating their own collections. These collections include books, music, images and moving images.

Figure 4.1   The Internet Archive

Academic subject guides

The services dealt with here follow academic classification schemes and cater specifically to academic researchers. They organize material according to disciplines and specialist areas within those disciplines. These guides have come under pressure from two directions in recent years and are becoming less and less popular. In the first place, keyword search engines have become much more sophisticated in predicting the search requirements of individual users, with the consequence that it has become much easier to identify materials in your subject area through searches on Google or Bing or Yahoo. In the second place, social networks, blogs and Web 2.0 and 3.0 content on services such as Amazon have generated new kinds of specialized subject guides that are much more focused than the big academic subject guides. The guides to 'Top Ten blogs' on various topics provided on blogs.com (**www.blogs.com/topten/**) includes many useful guides to key blogs on academic topics. A blog on social theory managed by several academics working in the area can provide a much more sophisticated and up-to-date guide to key texts and services than any guide with universal ambitions can hope to do. Nonetheless, the big academic subject guides remain useful in the kind of mapping exercises that researchers need to do when they begin a new project, providing a good starting point for an exploration of key online resources in a new research area.

Guides to academic resources

The Virtual Library (**www.vlib.org**) The World Wide Web Virtual Library is the original guide to academic subject guides, established in 1991. The Virtual Library appears to the user as a single organization, providing hundreds of guides on a vast array of subjects. It is effectively an umbrella title covering guides which vary widely in quality and which are nearly all produced by different individuals and organizations. Some of the Virtual Library guides are huge complex services in their own right, such as the Virtual Library on Sociology (**socserv2.mcmaster.ca/w3virtsoclib**), which catalogues a huge range of materials in Sociology including research centres, discussion lists and curricular resources. The areas covered by the guides are determined by those who create them and, as a result, coverage is very uneven. Those who produce the guides have to sign up to certain minimal common standards.

BUBL Information Service (**www.bubl.ac.uk**) Primarily aimed at the UK academic community, this service classifies resources according to the Dewey subject classification system used in many libraries. You can search by subject category and classification number. It focuses on major resources and provides short and precise descriptions of sites, but from 2011 it is no longer being updated.

Infomine (**infomine.ucr.edu**) Infomine is the Scholarly Internet Resource Collections produced by librarians from several campuses in the University of California system. It is extremely well organized. Entries are classified by subject area and are given associated keywords. It is organized by subject, including a category for 'Social Sciences and Humanities'. You can browse the subject categories and you can also search by keyword. It provides short descriptions of the sites it links to.

Internet Public Library 2 (**www.ipl.org**) A guide to Internet resources that have been evaluated by librarians. It has a heavy emphasis on academic sources and includes 'Arts and Humanities' and 'Social Science' sections. The Index focuses on key sites and provides useful short descriptions of every site included.

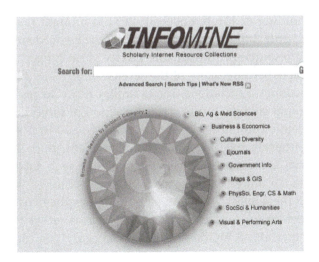

Figure 4.2   Infomine image

Professional Associations Academic professional associations sometimes provide guides to online resources in their subject area. Many of these associations also have specialist groups and some of these also provide guides to online resources in their area of specialization. You can identify the relevant associations through the links in the Intute directories (**www.intute.ac.uk**) or through the guide to professional associations provided by the *Scholarly Societies Project* (**www.scholarly-societies.org**). Perhaps the quickest way to identify relevant professional associations is to ask fellow-researchers what they regard as the key associations in your subject field.

H-Net (**www.h-net.org**) The H-Net discussion lists cover a range of areas in the social sciences and the humanities. All of the lists have websites and many of them provide guides to online resources in their area. These guides are particularly valuable because of the subject expertise involved, the focus on academic resources and the focus on major key resources.

Wikipedia (**www.wikipedia.org**) Wikipedia entries generally include a list of recommended websites. In many cases these are either guides to online resources on the topic in question or key sites on the topic. You have to remain aware, however, that there isn't the same level of quality control as there is in the organized academic guides described above.

Other guides There is also a huge range of focused academic guides set up by academics and institutions that do not belong to any wider service. One example is the Sociosite service (**www.sociosite.net**) based at the University of Amsterdam which is relevant both to Sociology and to a range of related social science disciplines

Intute (www.intute.ac.uk) and the decline of online subject catalogues

When public funding of Intute ended in 2011 it brought to an end one of the most careful and ambitious attempts to provide an academic subject catalogue of online resources. Although the service is no longer being updated, it remains valuable because many of the services it provides (listing key journals and professional associations, for example) relate to resources that are not subject to rapid change. Intute was a collection of subject directories that served the academic community in the UK but was, and is, freely available to everyone. In gathering together links to the relevant journals, professional associations, data sources and article collections in each subject area, these directories do much more than provide a set of hyperlinks – they provide an introduction to the subject areas and sub-disciplines they cover. Intute concentrated on identifying key resources in major areas rather than producing guides to very specialized topics. In each sub-category you can 'filter results' by 'resource type'.

Resource types include 'Research Projects/Centres', linking you to academic research units specializing in the relevant area, and 'Papers/Reports/Articles/Texts', which links you to major collections of full-text articles in the area. 'Bibliographical material' points you to specialized subject databases that are often unknown to anyone outside the field.

Each record contains a description of the resource linked to and a set of key-words for that resource. Many of the subject sections were maintained by aca-demic institutions or organizations which have an expertise in the subject area and you can restrict a keyword search to a particular subject category.

Search strategy

Exploring academic subject guides

Exploring a few major guides to online resources in your research area provides a way to quickly identify key online resources. For a research project on the politics of international football, you might begin by looking for a guide to online resources on the sociology of sport, a broad area that covers your topic. Because this is such a clearly demarcated, and popular, subject area, it is easy to find a guide by checking the *Intute: Social Sciences* guide where there is a category called 'The sociology of sport and leisure'. You can filter entries in this category to create lists of journals, blogs and associations. It identifies several key journals in this area, and an email list on the topic.

It includes a link to the *International Sociology of Sport Association* (ISSA). Professional associations like this generally provide guides to resources in their area and the ISSA section turns out to be a focused collection of online resources on the sociology of sport. It includes links to sociology of sport journals not included in the Intute guide as well as links to the *North American Society for the Sociology of Sport*, to research centres on 'sport and society' and to a 'Scholarly Sport site' that acts as a guide to academic resources on sport in general. The *North American Society* site in turn includes a blog that is used to distribute information on jobs, conferences and scholarships related to the sociology of sport, and provides its own guide to online resources.

All of these guides provide links to research centres and some of these centres in turn provide guides of their own to online resources in the area. In addition, some of them provide archives of publications by members of staff and an eclectic set of materials on the subject that can be of use to a researcher.

You can continue to search for related resources in the other academic subject guides, but this quick sweep through guides identified via Intute has already turned up a number of key resources that are listed in several different guides.

(Continued)

(Continued)

Flexibility is important in this search. It is not a matter of exhaustively exploring every resource listed in every guide, but of hopping from guide to guide, identifying two or three new resources in each guide, and using the guides themselves to identify other guides. It doesn't especially matter where your search begins or ends. There is a huge amount of overlap between all of these guides and you will quickly reach the point of diminishing returns.

The result of this exploration is a list of around ten major online academic resources, ranging from a specialist bibliography through mailing lists and blogs to journals, professional associations and key research centres. When you begin to do keyword searches of the open Web through the big search engines you will find that many of the hits you bring back will come from these key sites. Quickly getting to know the key resources in your area will make subsequent keyword searching much easier and faster.

If your subject area is as clearly titled and demarcated as 'sociology of sport' is, a simple keyword search on one of the big search engines can often provide a perfectly good starting point for exploring guides on the topic. A Google search on "sociology of sport", for example, brings back tens of thousands of hits, but among the first ten results are several of the key resources in the area, including the Intute section on 'sociology of sport'. Because the search term is used in the title of subject guides, research centres, journals and professional associations, these large and popular sites come to the top of the search results.

Universal subject guides

The Internet is full of subject directories that partition the entire world of human knowledge into browseable subject headings. Their ambitions are universal, aiming to guide you to everything from cars and holidays to zoology and astrophysics. Because they cover a lot, it's difficult for them to cover any one thing particularly well. The best of these guides come into their own in providing lists of things which fall naturally into list form, like sports teams, newspapers, universities or towns – anything that can be easily classified and categorized.

The main problem with these guides is that they exercise minimal quality control and include links of very poor quality, barely relevant to the category they've been included in. They often miss the central resources on a particular subject because they make no attempt to be comprehensive. They generally provide no description or minimal description of the resources they link to and they don't emphasize academic resources. Having said all this, it is well worth while to quickly trawl the two major directories listed below to find sub-sections related to the topic you're interested in, but only after you have used the academic guides listed above. Unlike the academic guides, they often have sections on very specialized and obscure topics if those topics also happen to be of great public concern and interest.

Yahoo! Directory (**dir.yahoo.com**) When you search the Yahoo Directory, the results at the top of the page are Yahoo subject categories that include your search term. These are followed by individual web pages that are catalogued in the Directory. Only a tiny proportion of web pages have been included in the Directory but it is still vast. Every category within Yahoo has its own web page. Each of these pages contains links to external web pages which fit into that category, and links to Yahoo sub-categories within that category. Only at the very bottom of the Yahoo subject tree will you find pages that only have external links. At the higher levels, category pages consist primarily of links to sub-categories. 'Social Science' is one of the main top-level categories in Yahoo. It has over 40 sub-categories. The numbers after the name of a category indicates how many links are included in that category. This includes the total number of all links within the sub-categories that come under that category. The higher-level categories are not necessarily the best sources of good links. Cataloguers put resources in the lowest-level category they can.

Many sub-categories fit into several different higher-level categories. The way Yahoo deals with this is to try to include sub-categories in all of the higher-level categories they belong to. Thus the Yahoo 'Peace and Conflict Studies' page includes a link to the sub-category 'Regional conflicts'. There is an @ sign after the name of the sub-category. This indicates that it is listed here for convenience but that it is actually located on another branch of the Yahoo subject tree, in this case the 'Politics' branch. External links are frequently listed in two different categories. As a result, certain categories in entirely different branches of the subject tree are almost identical in their contents.

Yahoo provides several national versions of its service. Yahoo UK and Ireland (**uk.yahoo.com**) and Yahoo Germany (**de.yahoo.com**) were among the first. The subject categories are generally the same as in the main Yahoo version but with additional categories and sub-categories of special relevance to the country concerned and additional links to sites relevant to the country. You have the option to limit your

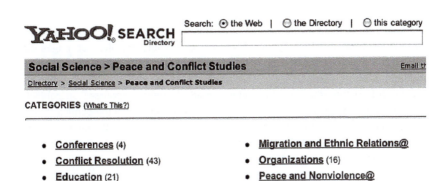

Figure 4.3 Yahoo 'Peace and Conflict Studies' category

search to sites related to the country involved. If you are searching for material in a language other than English, you should certainly search Yahoo for the country where that language is the main language. Sites in languages other than English are generally not included in the main Yahoo Directory if there is a national Yahoo where that language is the main language.

The Open Directory Project (**dmoz.org**) The Open Directory looks very similar to Yahoo but there is a major difference. Volunteers maintain the directory categories. This creates problems but it also means that many of the Open Directory categories are maintained by enthusiastic experts who know quite a bit about their area. The contents of the categories and even the categories themselves are very different from those in the Yahoo Directory. The Open Directory uses the same kind of subject tree structure as Yahoo and its layout is very similar. When you search Google Directory (**directory.google.com**), you search the contents of the Open Directory. If you choose to search it via Google, you will get a lot more results and a more sophisticated search, but this can sometimes make it more difficult to identify the relevant categories.

Search strategy

Exploring the universal subject guides

The universal subject guides don't generally include specialized academic guides but they provide many excellent guides to issues of current controversy and debate.

The construction by Israel of a 'Separation barrier' in the Palestinian territories under Israeli occupation is exactly the kind of current issue that the universal guides deal with well. There are two general approaches to identifying a guide to online resources on this issue. The first is to do a broad keyword search to identify the relevant categories in the guides that might include material on this topic. The second is to search on a term uniquely associated with your subject to pull up very specific web pages catalogued in the directory. These then point you to the relevant category they have been classified under.

The Open Directory (**dmoz.org**) includes a guide to online resources on conflict in Israel/Palestine. This guide provides a long list of other guides on the conflict that can be explored in turn. It also includes a section on the 'Occupation' that includes one item dealing directly with the barrier. A search in the Yahoo Directory on **Israel** brings up several categories but none of them seems directly relevant. A search on **"west bank barrier"**, on the other hand, brings up numerous results that belong to a Yahoo category entirely devoted to the 'Israeli West Bank Barrier'. This category provides a very useful starting point for exploration.

Wikipedia has good academic coverage in many areas but it can also be an excellent source of guides to topics of public debate. A search in Wikipedia on **"west bank barrier"** brings up an entry which points to the Wikipedia entry on 'Israeli West Bank barrier' (see Figure 4.4). This is a long article summarizing the political debates around the issue. At the end of the article there is a well-organized list of online resources on the topic, which acts as an excellent and extensive guide. It is significantly more useful than either the Yahoo or Open Directory guides on the same topic and includes virtually all of the resources identified by both of these, along with several others.

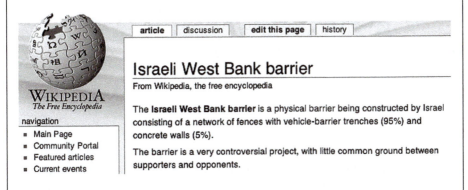

Figure 4.4   Extract from wikipedia entry on 'Israeli West Bank barrier'

About.com This provides a collection of several hundred subject guides, organized by subject category. A large number of the guides relate to areas of current political controversy, and these are to be found under the 'News and Issues' subject heading. Some of the guides are run by individuals who often put a personal stamp on the guide. Others look like a set of search engine results. About.com has direct authority over the guides it provides, commissioning guides on particular subjects, trying to ensure the guides have the same basic format and are all part of a single, coherent service. As a commercial company whose priorities are not shaped by academic research interests, it has few guides to obscure areas of academic interest. Some of the guides are rich in description of the sites they link to but they vary widely in quality.

Understanding web addresses

The URL or web address can quickly reveal information about a document that it would take much longer to find out by other means and can help you to assess documents quickly. They are essential to understanding how websites are organized.

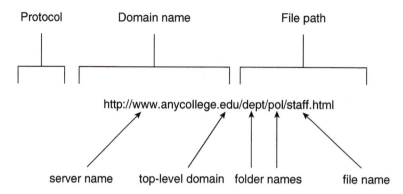

Figure 4.5 The structure of a Web address

Protocol

The first part of any web address is the protocol. The protocol used for web pages is the HyperText Transfer Protocol (http) so web addresses generally begin with **http://**. The ://separates the protocol from the rest of the address. Some URLs begin with **https://**. This indicates that there is an extra level of encryption at this site to facilitate secure and confidential communication, such as credit card transactions.

Among the other major protocols you will encounter are **rss://**, **gopher://**, **telnet://** and **ftp://**. RSS, indicating a link to a news feed, is the only one of these that most Internet users will regularly encounter. The other protocols are still used but they were much more important during an earlier stage of the Internet, before the World Wide Web existed. The main web browsers will automatically add **http://** to the start of any address you type in if you have not done so already.

Domain name

The domain name is the main part of any URL. The domain names are intended to be descriptive and to provide information about the service you are connecting to. A single computer may host thousands of domain names.

The domain name shown in Figure 4.5 illustrates the way in which these addresses are composed. The last part of the domain name is the top-level domain (see below) – **.edu** in the example in Figure 4.5, indicating that this is a US university. The middle part, **anycollege**, is the name of the imaginary university. The first part, **www**, is the server name or host name. It could just as easily be called 'Fred' or 'Matilda', and some of them are. Note that while the domain name is not case sensitive, the file path that follows it is.

Technical information: IP addresses

Every computer connected directly to the Internet (that is, not through another computer via a modem) has a unique IP address consisting of four sets of numbers, such as 127.131.10.176. The computer's domain name is just an alias for this number. In routing messages and requests across the Internet, it is these numbers that are used. They are the 'real' address.

When you make a request for a web page at a certain domain the first thing your computer has to do is look up the 'real' address for this domain name. It checks the nearest DNS server (Domain Name System), which keeps tables of the IP addresses.

Top-level domains

The last part of a domain name is the top-level domain. It tells you what country the computer is registered in or, in many cases, what type of organization runs the computer. 'Country code' top-level domains are often easy to guess, such as **.ca** for Canada, **.jp** for Japan, **.ru** for Russia. There is a top-level domain for every country in the world and a list is available online (**www.iana.org/domains/root/db/**). They always consist of two letters. 'Generic' top-level domains, by contrast, have three letters and tell you what type of organization runs the web server you have connected to. They reflect the US origins of the Internet. The US government, US universities and the US military were heavily involved in the development of the Net at the initial stages. As a result, they each got their own top-level domain.

Thus **.mil** is the top-level domain for the US military and the US military alone. **.edu** is short for educational institution, but the only educational institutions that use this top-level domain are US universities. **.gov** stands for government, the US government. Things are a little less clear-cut in the case of the other category domains. **.com** stands for commercial sites and while a huge proportion of **.com** domains are US-based, anyone, anywhere in the world can easily get a **.com** address. **.org** was intended to be the domain for non-commercial organizations but is now open to everyone. It includes political parties in countries outside the USA as well as international organizations and non-governmental organizations (NGOs). **.int** is theoretically for international organizations but some of the largest of these are in the **.org** domain, including the United Nations and the OSCE (Organization for Security and Cooperation in Europe). NATO, on the other hand, uses the **.int** domain. **.net** was intended for organizations concerned with the administration and development of the Internet, but anyone can now get a **.net** address. Virtually all Internet Service Providers (ISPs) and all free web space providers use the **.com** domain. Lots of small organizations use web space provided by one or other of these sources and therefore the web addresses end in .com. Just because their web addresses include .com does not mean that they are commercial sites. .us is the country domain for the USA, but the vast majority of US sites do not use this domain. During the past few years an increasing number of new generic top-level domains have been approved, among them **asia**, **cat**, **jobs** and **travel**.

People all over the world can register in the domains **.int**, **.org**, and **.com**, but a large proportion of those outside the USA register in their country domains. The country domains are complicated as well. Just because a computer is registered in a certain country does not mean it is located in that country. Certain poorer countries that have domain names that are commercially attractive have taken to selling names to the highest bidder, no matter where they are based. There is no guarantee that a domain ending in **.tm** is actually located in Turkmenistan, for example. The central Asian republic has been selling domain names to US companies who treat the **.tm** as short for trademark. Likewise, the tiny pacific island nation of Tonga is not actually home to the many websites which have registered there simply for the purpose of having a domain name ending in **.to**, such as **come.to**, **welcome.to** and so on.

Several countries outside the USA have set up organizational domains of their own within the country domain. Thus the UK has **ac.uk** (academic community, i.e. universities), **co.uk** (commercial companies) and **gov.uk** (the UK government). In Australia, **edu.au** is for universities, **org.au** for organizations. Japan has **go.jp** for government sites and **ac.jp** for universities.

Technical information: port numbers

Sometimes you will come across a domain name that includes an odd-looking number, like **www.anycollege.edu:80**. This is a port number. A web server can allow access through several different ports. When you connect to the domain name on its own with no number, you connect through the default port (usually port 80). Some webmasters used to add the port number to their web address to make doubly sure people could connect, but this is no longer very common.

The path

After the domain name comes the path, **/depts/pol/staff.html** in the example in Figure 4.5 above. The path, as its name suggests, lays out a path to the particular file you want. Each forward slash separates one folder from another until the last item, which is the name of the file you want to retrieve, in this case, **staff.html**.

When you connect to the address in the example in Figure 4.5, your computer essentially asks the web server, 'Please open the folder **depts**, then open the folder **pol** which is inside it. In that is a file called **staff.html**. Please send it to me.' You can often tell quite a lot from the path. Here, for example, it seems likely that **staff.html** is a list of staff in the politics department.

Understanding websites

The website to which a document belongs provides the context within which that document can be understood, situating it as part of a collection of related documents. To use a web page without knowing what site it belongs to can be a bit like using a photocopied page without knowing anything about the book it is copied from. Understanding how websites are organized is essential to understanding the context of the materials that you find online. It will also help you to make much more efficient use of both the subject guides and the keyword search engines.

Defining site

'Website' is not as simple a concept as 'book'. A website may well be the online equivalent of a book, with the various chapters organized as separate web pages. It might equally be the equivalent of a magazine, a journal, an archive or a collection of any of these. A site may take full advantage of the potential of hypertext and be organized in a way for which there is not even a remote equivalent in print. A broad definition of 'website' might describe it as consisting of all of the materials placed together on the Web by a particular organization or project or individual. The central question is 'whose' site you are looking at. Sites, thus defined, can be massive. The Boston College site (**www.bc.edu**), the Irish government site (**www.irlgov.ie**), the US House of Representatives site (**www.house.gov**), all contain numerous sub-sections. It can also mean a tiny collection of documents put on the Web by a single individual or even a single document if it is genuinely not part of any larger organizing structure. The key element is authority.

Most large organizational sites consist of thousands of documents organized in many different sub-sections. It is often necessary to identify the particular sub-section of a site to which a document belongs in order to understand it fully. Thus, to understand a document on the 'anycollege' site called 'list of courses', it is necessary to know if it is part of the law department section of the site, or the department of history section or if, indeed, it is just part of the 'anycollege' site as a whole, providing a full list of courses for the entire college.

A more narrow way to define 'site' is to say that a site is a clearly distinct collection of materials. That is, although it may be part of a larger site, and although it may have no independence or separate authority, it does have a distinct identity. By this definition, site is the lowest level of the organizing framework within which a document is located. This is the level that provides most information about the context in which a document exists.

Higher levels of organizations are included in the name you give to the lowest level of organization. For example, if an article on human rights law in East Timor belongs to a collection called 'human rights archive' run by the law department at 'anycollege', then the site to which the document belongs is 'human rights archive of law department, anycollege'. Site, defined as the lowest level of the organizing framework, has certain key characteristics. It should have a home page that provides information about that site and provides access to an index of materials on that site. A site should have its own title clearly stated on its home page.

Search strategy

Exploring a website

Because websites differ so much in how they are organized, every new website you come across can be fairly described as an 'unfamiliar research environment' (Basch, 1998: 182). There is a traditional research approach to such environments that can usefully be adapted and applied to websites.

1. Identify the starting point

When you come across a useful document identify the home page of the site it belongs to. Most of those designing websites design them for users who enter through the home page and this is the best starting point for exploration of a site.

2. Identify the boundaries of the site

Scan the URLs of the links on the home page. Determine which links are internal, leading to other items on this site, and which are external, linking to documents at other sites. Follow the main internal links that seem relevant to your work until they either lead outside the service or end in substantive documents or document collections.

3. Identify which parts of the site are relevant to you

You will do this in the process of identifying the site boundaries.

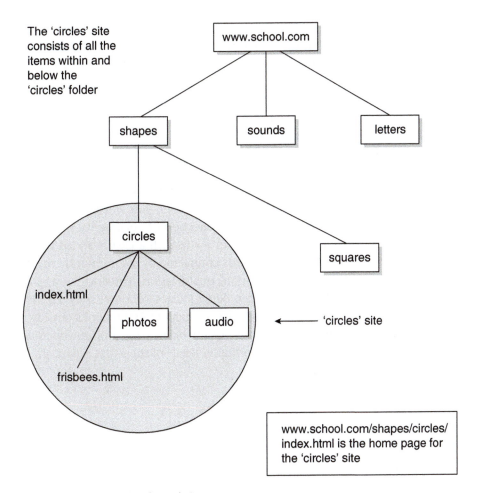

Figure 4.6 The structure of a website

Site and URLs

URLs can provide a lot of information about how a site is organized and how documents are related to each other. Most folders on websites contain an index document that acts as a home page for that folder. To get a good idea of how a site is organized, look at the index pages for the various folders.

www.school.edu/shapes/circles/frisbees.html

The URL above links to a document about frisbees. The document is in a folder called **circles**, suggesting that **Frisbees.html** is part of a collection of documents about circles or objects shaped like circles. To see the index page for that folder, just 'hack back the URL' by deleting the file name (the last part of the address) and going to **www.school.edu/shapes/circles/**.

When a URL ends in a folder name rather than a file name, your browser automatically looks for a file in the folder called **index.html** or **index.htm** (**htm** is often used as the file extension for a web page instead of **html**). This will usually act as a sort of home page for that folder. Some people use a different name for the index page in their folder and if you do not get any result using the folder name, you can try adding some of the names commonly used, such as **default.html**, **home.html**, **contents.html** or **toc.html** (table of contents).

If there is no index page in the lowest level folder, go up a level and see if there is one there. In the example given here, try **www.schools.edu/shapes/**, and if that produces nothing go back up to the domain name **www.schools.edu**.

If you do find an index page in the **circles** folder, you will have to decide if it constitutes the home page of a distinct collection of documents. If it presents itself as a home page or an index page for a site with a clearly stated title, if it provides access to an index of documents connected by a common theme, then it is a site home page, with one important qualification. The documents should be hosted on this site itself, rather than being located on other sites. This is not to say a home page will link only to pages in that site, but its links outside that site are generally external links and it is not the home page for those documents except in rare cases. It will also link to higher levels of the site it is part of.

Exercises

Exercise 1: Exploring academic subject guides

1 Identify a guide to resources in the broad subject area your research topic belongs to. Use this guide as a starting point to identify at least three other guides in the same subject area.
2 Use these guides to identify at least five key online resources relevant to your research as quickly as possible, including at least one of each of the following:

   o A mailing list / discussion list or Blog
   o A professional association / scholarly society
   o A research centre or institute
   o An academic journal.

Exercise 2: Searching a universal subject guide

Identify a topic of public debate and current interest related to your research topic. Search for guides on the topic in the following services:

- The Open Directory (**dmoz.org**)
- Yahoo Directory (**dir.yahoo.com**)
- Wikipedia (**www.wikipedia.org**)

1 Briefly describe your experience of searching each of these services.
2 Assess the quality and usefulness of the guides they provide.
3 List at least five key resources identified through these guides.

Exercise 3: Analyzing web addresses

Identify the URL of a web page relevant to your research. The URL path should include at least two folders after the domain name.

1 Analyse the URL, explaining what each component tells you about the web page and the site it belongs to.
2 'Hack back' the URL and try to identify index pages in each folder and an index page for the domain.
3 Describe the results of these attempts.

Exercise 4: Exploring a website

Identify a key website in your subject area that is of use in your research. Explore all sections of the site.

1 Briefly describe the contents of the site.
2 List the main section or sections of the site that are of use to you and give the URL for this section or sections.

FIVE
Searching the keyword search engines

Introduction

The search engine wars are over and Google has won, for the time being at least. In the course of the past few years Google has moved from being the largest and most popular search engine to being, in certain important ways, the only search engine, far ahead of its closest competitors, Bing and Yahoo. This dominance is seriously challenged in China, however, where a variety of Chinese-language search engines, chief among them Baidu, present a challenge to Google's global domination. By spring 2010 Google's share of the global search engine market was 86 per cent while its closest rival, Yahoo, had less than 7 per cent, although Google's dominance was not quite as marked in the USA, where Yahoo and Bing together accounted for 30 per cent of searches by 2011 (Goodwin, 2011). This marked the peak of a steady rise in the dominance of Google, reflected in the fact that the verb 'googling' has been widely accepted as a synonym for searching the Internet. When Microsoft once again relaunched their search engine in 2009, rebranded this time as Bing, US comedian Stephen Colbert joked that 'Bing is a great website for doing Internet searches. I know that, because I Googled it.'

The sophistication of Google provides much of the explanation for its success, but it is a sophistication that is making it increasingly difficult to talk in terms of a Google search. Google draws on data, including your location and your search history, to predict the kind of results (and advertizements) you might be interested in. In doing this, they are drawing on the many thousands of searches that each of us now carry out every year. The outcome is that two people sitting side by side might get entirely different search results for the same query. No longer can we say 'this is what Google will retrieve' in response to a particular query.

What Google retrieves, and the related sites that Google-powered services such as YouTube suggest you look at, depends on the search history of the person who is entering the query. The great advantage of this is that Google's guesses as to what you might be interested in have become increasingly accurate and the work of the searcher has become ever easier. Where once we modified and elaborated our queries subtly to bring certain results to the top, now Google does much of that work for us, suggesting related searches that might be productive, attempting to complete our query for us before we have even finished typing, and even correcting our spelling for us. Yahoo and Bing similarly customize the results, albeit in different ways.

Many people do all of their Internet searching through the big search engines and it's easy to see why. You'll usually find something useful on your topic reasonably quickly through Google or Bing or Yahoo. There are problems with the search engines, however. It's easy to be swamped with results and it's tempting to resolve this problem by using a few of the items on the first page or two of results even if these are not the highest quality, the most relevant or the most important materials on the subject. It can also be much more difficult to understand and evaluate documents when they are presented out of context as isolated search results.

You will use the search engines for a range of tasks from the very beginning, but you will be able to search them much more effectively after you have explored the academic literature on your subject and the major online resources in your area. Searching with this experience behind you, you will find that you will already be familiar with many of the sources that appear in your search results and that you will have a much better understanding of the context for the documents your searches pull up. You should also have built up a store of search terms unique to your subject that will allow you to devise specialized queries. The most important knowledge for devising effective search queries is knowledge of your specialized research topic, not knowledge of the search engines.

We tend to think of the search engines as windows on to the Internet, but they also play a powerful role in shaping what we see when we search. The algorithms, the complex mathematical formulae used to decide how to order the search results, often push the most powerful organizations and the most popular sites to the top of the results pages, even though these may not necessarily be the most relevant results. This reinforces the power of the larger sites and ensures that they are far more visible than those on the margins. In addition, it is possible for people to 'game' the ranking system used by Google in order to ensure that their websites are pushed to the top or closer to the top of the search results, at least temporarily. In this way the search engines can reinforce offline inequalities in power and visibility. When Google complied in 2006 with Chinese government requests to block politically sensitive sites in their new Chinese search service, it provided a stark illustration of the powerful role the search engines play in shaping what we see. Mashable (**mashable.com**), the most popular social and digital media blog, covers major new developments relating to the big search engines, while Search Engine Land (**searchengineland.com**) provides specialized coverage focused on the search engines. Wikipedia pages dealing with the search engines are also a good source of regular updates on changes to the major search engines and information on studies comparing the search engines.

The big three

This section examines in detail the three major search engines – Google, Yahoo and Bing. Yahoo is now powered by Bing and there is a huge overlap in the search results they generate. There are minor differences in how they present results and, given that they are the second and third most popular search engines, they are dealt with separately here. Many long-established search engines have fallen by the wayside during the past two to three years but a few are still limping along, falling further behind Google as time passes. They are not dealt with in detail here. Most of them are connected in one way or another with Google or Bing in any case. Thus, AOL search takes search results from Google. Because these other search engines search the same indexes in slightly different ways, they will pull up different results, but the overlap with the big three is so great that there is no need to search the others separately.

All of the search engines index billions of web pages but it's not possible to directly compare the size of the indexes because they each count the number of items in their index in significantly different ways. Having said this, Google has clearly had the largest index for several years past. Size isn't everything though. If you only need three or four good results, the most important thing is that they come to the top of your search results. It doesn't really matter if the long tail of unused results contains 10,000 or 40,000 hits, and both Yahoo and Bing give Google a run for its money in terms of the relevance of results.

Judging website popularity

Type the URL for a website into *Alexa* (**www.alexa.com**) to get statistics on how popular the site is, on the demographics of those who visit the site, on the number of other sites that link to it, and on the search queries that most frequently bring users to the site in

(Continued)

(Continued)

Figure 5.1 Alexa image

question. They also provide information on the education level, gender and age profile of visitors to websites and whether they are accessing them from home or work. They also show you the extent to which visitors have a different demographic profile to web users in general and allow you to compare two or more sites. *Compete* (**www.compete.com**) is another service that performs many of the same functions.

Despite their vast size, none of the search engines comes close to covering the entire Web. There is a huge overlap between the search engine indexes, but all of them include millions of results not available in any of the others. If you are carrying out a 'needle in the haystack' search, it is well worth using two of the major search engines. One of the other big search engines will frequently turn up results for your query that were not available in Google. And because they use different criteria for ranking pages, a search on the same search terms in two of these search engines can retrieve radically different results, despite the massive overlap.

Google, Bing and Yahoo all search Word documents, pdf files, PowerPoint and Excel files and others as well as web pages. The simple search facilities that many websites provide on their own pages often do not search these kinds of files and you can find materials on a website by searching the search engines that you will not find by searching the site directly.

If you enter more than one word as a search query the search engines treat it as an AND query and will only return documents that contain all of these words. Google will give higher ranking to pages that include your search terms as an exact phrase. The order in which you type search terms will also affect the search results.

The search engines do not distinguish between capital and lower-case letters. If you search for **Snow White** you will get results for both **Snow White** and **snow white**.

Most of the search engines do not provide search 'stemming'. That is, they will search for the exact search term but not for related words using the same 'stem'. If you want results on **child** and **children**, you have to enter both terms into the search box. Google provides a limited form of stemming, searching for certain variations on your search terms.

Google (www.google.com)

Google pioneered a ranking system that gives greatest prominence to web pages that a lot of other popular web pages link to. This ranking system is directly modelled on the citation ranking system by which academic journal articles are judged according to the number of other academic articles that cite them. The most linked-to, and often, as a result, the most important, central and significant sites related to a query, come to the top of the results list. Click on 'more search tools' to the left of the Google search results to filter your search by location and date. The maximum length for a search query in Google is ten words. Words after the tenth word will be ignored.

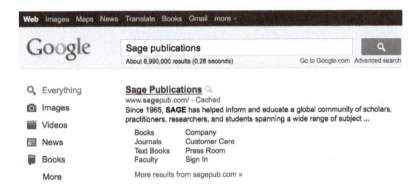

Figure 5.2 Google search result

Bing (bing.com)

Bing ranks pages according to the relevance of the contents to your search terms and the number of other popular or highly regarded web pages that link to it. Bing's ranking system assesses both popularity and relevance, just as Google does, but it uses different methods. As a result, it can generate radically different results for the same query. It displays your search history to the left of the search results, allowing you to move easily to sites that you have looked at recently. When you run your mouse over a search result in Bing you get access to a 'More on this page' box which provides a limited preview of the page so that you can quickly decide whether it is useful to you.

Figure 5.3 Bing search image

Yahoo (www.yahoo.com)

Yahoo draws on the Bing database but there are slight differences between the search results they generate for the same queries. The advanced search is available under 'More' or 'Options'.

Advanced searching

Each of the three major search engines provides an advanced search page. In all three, the 'Advanced search' option becomes available after you have done an initial search. Many of the options on the advanced search pages can be entered directly into the standard search boxes if you know the equivalent search terms. The following features are available in the three major search engines, unless stated otherwise.

Search for the exact phrase

You can do this in the standard search box by using quotation marks (for example, "outrageous assault"). This is the single most powerful way to make your query more precise.

Restrict by language

If you use English language search terms, the overwhelming majority of documents you pull up will be in English. It's not necessary to exclude other languages unless you find that there is a confusingly large number of non-English hits. If you're searching for documents in another language, however, you'll often find your search terms pull up a large number of English-language documents which happen to contain your search term for some reason, simply because such a huge proportion of web documents are in English. In this case, it can be useful to limit your search to the language you are interested in.

Restrict by date

Yahoo allow you to restrict your search to materials updated during the last three months, six months or year, while Google allows you to restrict it to the last 24 hours, week, month or year. Select 'More search tools' to the left of the Google search results and then the 'Custom range' option to limit your search to pages updated between two specific dates. If you're researching an event, you can restrict your search to materials that were indexed by the search engine in the few days surrounding that event. If you are running a specialized query again several months after you first searched, this can be useful in excluding some of the results you picked up in earlier searches. If you limit the search to the last three months, you will pick up plenty of documents that are one or two years old, presumably because some minor element in these pages has been changed in the meantime.

Displaying results

Search engines traditionally displayed ten results per page. Google and Yahoo allow you to display up to a hundred results per page. Sometimes you will be searching not for a single document but for all occurrences of a particular phrase. In these cases you may well be interested in all of the results returned, and this option will allow you to move much more quickly through the results.

Restrict by location

All three search engines allow you to limit your search by 'country' or 'region'. This is a much more effective way of restricting your search geographically than limiting your search by site/domain which is also possible. Restricting your search to the top-level domain of a particular country does not limit your search to websites operating from that country because so many people register their sites in domains other than those of the country in which they're based, and because not everyone in a country chooses to register their site under the top-level domain for that country.

File formats

Yahoo and Google allow you to restrict your search to certain file formats. You can limit your search to pdf documents (the format used for many published articles and reports), Word documents (used for many course outlines and bibliographies) or a range of other formats.

Restrict by site/domain

This allows you to restrict your search to documents from a particular site or domain. The more detail you provide, the more restricted your search. You don't need to use the advanced search page for this. Simply add **site:** to your query. Thus, **site:edu** restricts your search to US universities; **site:harvard.edu** restricts it to web servers at Harvard University; **site:www.ksg.harvard.edu** restricts it to documents on the Kennedy School of Government server at Harvard. Note that you can only include parts of the domain address and can't include any part of the file path. To include the file path, use the **inurl** option outlined below.

Searching URLs

This option allows you to limit your search to URLs. You might search for URLs that include **anthro**, for example, in the knowledge that this is a common abbreviation used in the URLs of anthropology departments. It can also be used to restrict a site search more tightly than is possible when you limit it by site. In a site search you can limit your search to **www.un.org**, the United Nations domain, but the URL search allows you to include all or part of the URL, not just the domain name. It allows you to search for **www.un.org/documents**, limiting your search to items in that particular folder on the UN site. Both Google and Yahoo allow you to carry out this search in the normal search box: **inurl:www.un.org/documents**, for example. You can also do this on the Google advanced search page, choosing 'in the URL of the page' from the options for 'Where your keywords show up'.

Searching titles

You can limit your search to the titles of web pages. This is available as an advanced option in Yahoo and Google (as an option for 'Where your keywords show up') but in all of the search engines you can search titles in the ordinary search box: **intitle:anthology**, for example.

Searching for links

The link search option available in Google ('Find pages that link to the page') limits your search to documents that link to a particular website or web page. You can also carry out this search in Google by typing **link** in the normal search box. **link:en. wikipedia.org** will return all pages everywhere which link to any document on the English-language version of Wikipedia. **link:en.wikipedia.org/wiki/Quaero**, on the other hand, returns every page on the Web which links to this Wikipedia entry on Quaero, the European search engine which was intended to rival Google and challenge the domination of American-owned search engines. This search has much in common with an academic citation search. If you find a key website in your area, or a very specialized website concerned directly with your research topic, searching for pages that link to it can provide a unique way of identifying directly related sites.

Table 5.1 Advanced search terms

Search term	Examples	Explanation
Intitle	intitle:theory	Returns documents whose title includes the word 'theory'.
Site	site:edu	Returns documents where the domain name ends in edu.
	site:anycollege.edu	Returns documents where the domain name ends in anycollege.edu.
Inurl	inurl:psych	Returns documents whose URL contains 'psych'.
Link	link:anycollege.edu	Returns documents which contain a hyperlink to a page whose URL includes anycollege.edu. In Bing and Yahoo you have to include http:// at the start of the address.
	link:anycollege.edu/ pol/index.html	Returns documents which contain a link to this exact URL.

Meta search engines

Meta search engines run your query on several search engines at the same time so you don't have to waste time visiting each of them individually. Several of them limit this to a joint search of the big three. Since all search engines have slightly different search syntax, some of the meta search engines simplify, crudely translating your query for search engines that don't understand it. Thus, in some of them, you cannot be as precise as you can when you go to a search engine directly.

Some of them also include a wide range of specialized databases in their search, emphasizing that they reach into parts of the 'invisible Web' that are not reached by the major search engines. Most of these vast databases have nothing to do with academic research and simply generate a confusingly large volume of results. Some of the best known of the meta search engines are listed below.

> *Beaucoup* (**www.beaucoup.com**) This allows you to search a wide range of specialized databases and the big search engines simultaneously.
> *Dogpile* (**www.dogpile.com**).
> *Metacrawler* (**www.metacrawler.com**) This allows you to search the major search engines. It eliminates duplicates.

Comparing search engines with meta search engines

A 'needle in the haystack' search in all of the major search engines and meta search engines reveals the large overlap between the major search engines but also shows that Bing and Yahoo are picking up results that Google doesn't. The search for "**CO 730**" **Archives Iraq mandate** was carried out in 2011. "**CO 730**" is the code for a British National Archive file on the British government mandate in Iraq in the 1930s. Relevant results are those that deal with the mandate and refer to this specific archive file.

Google returns 56 results, by far the largest number, but misses several of the results turned up by Yahoo (15 results) and Bing (13 results). Although Yahoo draws on the Bing database, Yahoo picks up nine results that Bing doesn't, while eight of the results returned by Bing are not picked up by Yahoo.

Searching Yahoo, Bing and Google simultaneously, *Dogpile* brought back 19 results for this specialized query, of which nine were not among the Google results while seven of them had been found *only* by Google. The fact that there is such disparity between the results brought back by the three major search engines indicates that it is well worth searching all three if you have a very specific query and you are concerned to pick up every scrap of information related to your query. Dogpile didn't bring back any results that couldn't be found by searching the search engines directly and it missed out on several items that were turned up by direct searches. There doesn't seem to be a strong argument for using the meta search engines in academic research, given that research queries will generally be quite specific and complex. When they simplify queries, the meta search engines hinder rather than help specialized searching.

Boolean searching

Named after an English mathematician called George Boole, who devised the basic principles on which it is based, Boolean searching is a small set of simple search terms. The main terms are AND, OR, NOT. Most search engines understand these search terms.

In addition, the search facilities on a lot of individual websites and huge numbers of online databases use Boolean terminology. If you learn the Boolean terms provided in Table 5.2, you will be able to use them in lots of situations.

You can use the **OR** term to search for variations on a word. Search for **Israel AND (Palestine OR Palestinian)**, for example. You can also use it to make a strict AND search a little bit looser: **revolution AND (communist OR socialist)**, for example. In Google you can omit the brackets.

Table 5.2 Boolean searching

Search term	Example	Explanation
AND	Israel AND Palestine	Documents containing both words
OR	Israel OR Palestine	Documents containing either word
NOT	Israel NOT Palestine	Documents containing Israel but not containing Palestine
AND NOT	Israel AND NOT Palestine	The same as NOT. Some search engines insist on AND NOT
NEAR	Israel NEAR Palestine	Documents containing both words but only if they appear within a few words of each other

Table 5.3 Math searching

Search term	Boolean equivalent	Example	Explanation
+	AND	+Palestine +Israel	Documents including the words Israel and Palestine
–	NOT	+Palestine –Israel	Documents including the word Palestine but not including the word Israel

The Boolean terms AND and NOT can be replaced by plus and minus signs in the major search engines, as illustrated in Table 5.3.

How search engines search

When you enter your query into a search engine it does not search the open Web. It searches the index to its own colossal database of web pages. This database is constantly updated by programs called 'robots' that trawl the open Web, following one hyperlink after another, adding each new document they locate to the database. The robots locate sites for inclusion by following the links in the web pages they have already indexed. If no other web page links to a web page, the search engines cannot find it unless someone sends them an email letting them know it exists. The speed at which they can work is determined by how fast they can send requests and process the documents they get back. After they retrieve the documents, there is a further time delay before they are indexed. Given the vast size of the Internet and the fact that documents change regularly, the search engine databases cannot possibly be kept up to date.

The search engines give priority to major sites and to rapidly changing sites such as news sources, but robots may not visit less prominent sites for months on end. In the meantime the site may have changed beyond recognition or have disappeared completely. The out-of-date information will stay in the search engine database until the robot visits the site again. This is the reason why search engines often bring up hits which don't exist and why they sometimes send you to documents that don't actually contain the keyword you used.

Google and Bing results provide a link to 'cached' web pages, allowing you to view the version of the document cached in their database (and possibly several months old) instead of seeing what's currently at that URL. In the case of a fast-changing site, the 'cached' document may actually be the one relevant to your query. The link to the cached page in Bing is at the bottom of the 'More on this page' pop-up box.

There are many online databases that the search engines don't cover, including databases of academic articles, newspapers and major organizations. The search engines cannot search any site that doesn't want to be searched. When a robot visits a site the first thing it has to do is request a file called *robots.txt*. If this file says robots are refused access, the robot can venture no further into the site.

Since the search engines can't hope to cover the entire web they have adopted a range of techniques to cope with this. In the case of large websites they will often index just a sample of pages and not even attempt to download the whole site. They only index a certain proportion of the full text of longer documents, the first 100k of a web page in the case of Google (roughly 70 pages of text). A large proportion of the web pages included in the Google databases have scarcely been indexed at all. Only their URLs and titles are indexed. The practical implications of these limitations are clear. When you do a 'needle in the haystack' search on the web for a very rare search term, you cannot be guaranteed of finding all uses of that term online, even if you use several search engines.

The fact that search engines often only sample sites emphasizes the importance of identifying the home pages of key sites and mining them thoroughly yourself. You can't rely on the search engine to have included every page on a site in its index.

Devising search queries

By the time you come to systematically use the big keyword search engines, you should already be familiar with the central resources and the core academic literature in your area. Your queries will be very specific, dealing with a range of specialized issues relevant to your topic. By this stage you will also have a well-developed knowledge of your subject area, know more or less what you're looking for in these searches, and have a rich store of keywords uniquely associated with your topic. All of these provide an essential base for effective searching. Start your search with a reality check, asking yourself who might put material related to your search topic online and why. This will give you a much better sense of the kinds of material you're hoping to find.

Flexibility is the key to efficient use of the big search engines. Think of a query as something that you develop and adapt. If your query does not turn up the required results in the first 10 or 20 hits, devise a new query and search again, and then devise another, and another. If the item you're looking for is in the fifth or sixth screen of hits, then effectively your search hasn't found it at all. It will take so long to work your way down to that screen that it is much more time-effective to change your search terms and do a fresh search.

There is no reason you shouldn't quickly run through four or five queries in the space of ten minutes. You might carry out four or five quick searches without investigating a single link. To do this you need to learn how to quickly assess the potential relevance of links by scanning and analyzing the information on the search results page. This involves getting to know the different genres of web page that exist, knowing the key sources in your area, understanding the URLs and having a good knowledge of your subject area.

Aim for a unique combination of words and phrases which is certain to appear in a document directly related to your topic but which could not possibly appear in other documents. It may sound ludicrously ambitious but it's not. If you can find the right search terms, two or three words in combination can be enough to exclude all but a few web pages. So much has been written and published in the English language over time that the language is replete with clichés. The result is that even apparently distinctive phrases occur in tens of thousands of web pages. 'Descent into chaos', for example, is an evocative and distinctive phrase but it is repeatedly used to describe a wide range of conflict situations, from Vietnam to Iraq. Google returns over 320,000 pages with this exact phrase while Yahoo returns over 360,000.

By contrast with this, an unusual combination of just a few words can be unique, even if they are not distinctively associated with the subject matter. The string of words 'pioneered a ranking' appeared in a sentence earlier in this chapter. This phrase generated just one result in Bing and five results in Google in 2011.

In the building of search queries certain kinds of words and word combinations are particularly useful. Several of these are dealt with here.

Quotes

To find discussion of a person's work, search for a few words from a frequently quoted phrase. To find a copy of a piece of written work, search for a short distinctive quote from the work. The quote does not have to be meaningful. If you are looking for the full text of *The Communist Manifesto* by Marx and Engels, for example, a search for the best known phrase from this work **"Workers of the World Unite"** will retrieve over 200,000 documents, only a tiny proportion of them copies of the *Manifesto*. If, on the other hand, you search for a meaningless but distinctive string of words from *The Communist Manifesto*, such as **"tale of the spectre"**, you are more likely to pull up the full text of the *Manifesto* (or parodies of it).

Names

The name of a person associated with a topic in a peripheral way, perhaps as a minor contributor to an event or project, can be extremely effective in locating very specific information, particularly if the person has a distinctive name. A search for **"Lenchen Demuth"**, housekeeper to the Marx family, for example, can retrieve materials directly concerned with the detail of Karl Marx's private life more effectively than a search using Marx's own name.

Place names

In certain cases, street names, villages, or the name of a particular building, lake or desert will be linked to your topic and to virtually no other topic. Even the most placeless and theoretical topics will often be associated with particular places – where an experiment was carried out, for example, or where an important centre or individual was based. If the place name is obscure, it can act as a term uniquely (or almost uniquely) associated with your subject. Add a broad term connected to your subject area to modify it sufficiently to cut out all the commercial references.

Common place names are less useful. Particularly if it is a large city or town in the USA, it will appear on tens or even hundreds of thousands of web pages. As a result, it may not act very effectively as a filter. The Internet abounds with lists of things organized geographically, lists of consulates or phone companies or shoe shops. Even the smallest country or region is included in dozens of such lists. Nonetheless, common place names can very effectively modify a search that is already quite specific.

Subject phrases

Every subject develops a distinctive terminology that you will become familiar with as your research proceeds and which can be used to ensure that search results relate to that subject area.

Search strategy

Building a query

An exploration of the way in which *The Lord of the Rings* has been invoked in relation to the 'War on Terror' might begin with a Google search on **"Lord of the Rings" "War**

(Continued)

(Continued)

on Terror". However, this search brings up almost a million results in Google, indicating that this seemingly obscure combination is much more prevalent than you might have expected. The results are hugely bloated because both phrases are also the titles of video games. **"Lord of the Rings" "War on Terror" -game** reduces the results dramatically, to around 245,000. Almost all of the links in the first page of results are directly relevant and provide leads to further debate. The search can be further refined by using a term which is directly associated with the drawing of parallels between *The Lord of the Rings* and the 'War on Terror'. Adding the surname of Viggo Mortensen, an actor in *The Lord of the Rings* films who drew such parallels, and who was at the centre of public controversy as a result, focuses the search on recent public debates on the parallels. The word **Mortensen** is not central to the subject at hand but in combination with the other two search terms, is uniquely associated with a specific public debate on the topic.

Restricting your search by site can be used to limit this search even further. Thus **"Lord of the Rings" "War on Terror" Mortensen site:edu** limits it to US university sites and turns up around 670 results. A search limited to UK academic sites (**"Lord of the Rings" "War on Terror" Mortensen site:ac.uk**) brings up only two results.

The key sites identified in these initial searches now provide a useful starting point for further searching.

Look before you leap

Certain common genres of web page appear frequently when you do searches on an academic topic. They seem tantalizingly relevant to your search but in the end are of no use. Titles, text extracts and URLs in the list of search results can together help you to decide what kind of document the link leads to without clicking on it. As you learn to recognize a wide range of document genres you can scan search results much more quickly and effectively. Among the most common genres are the following.

University course descriptions

There are now millions of course descriptions and syllabi online. They may include reading lists, an outline of topics to be covered, and a few paragraphs about the topic. As a result, they are packed with keywords related to a very specific subject. You can sometimes identify them because they'll have a course code in the title. If not, the URL will often reveal them as course descriptions. Look for course codes, names of faculty/staff and of departments, URLs like: **www.anycollege.edu/econ/Taylor/macro.html** or **www.anycollege.edu/psych/courses/py101.html**.

Bibliographical references

Publishers, booksellers, colleges and libraries all provide documents that consist solely of lists of books. It's easy to see how a long list of books on psychology, for example, could be densely packed with very specific and obscure keywords related to the subject. Once again, a combination of document title and URL will often tell you this with no need for you to check out the document itself.

Link pages

A long list of hyperlinks to sources on an academic subject will include lots of keywords relevant to the topic but may not contain anything of substance.

Search tip

Bookmarking queries

Most search engines will allow you to bookmark your queries. When you have developed a very effective query, bookmark the page of results it brings up. When you go to the bookmarked page a week or a month or a year later, it will automatically run your query again and bring up an up-to-date results page.

Technical difficulties

Contents lists

Many longer web pages begin with a contents list, a set of hyperlinks that point to various sub-sections of the page. URLs in the contents list will include the tell-tale # (the 'hash' sign). **frisbees.html#red**, for example, will link you to the part of **frisbees.html** dealing with red frisbees.

If you click on an item in the contents list before the whole document has downloaded, you will often be brought back to the top of the page. This happens when the part of the document it links you to has not yet downloaded.

Each time you click on a link in a contents list your browser treats it as a request for a new document even though you just want to go further down in this document. It's often quicker to scroll through the document. Each request you make for a sub-section of a document appears as a separate item in your history list and therefore as a separate step you have to take if you use the back arrow.

When 'back' doesn't work

You are looking at a web document. You click on back. The same web document appears. If you have not been using a contents list within that document there is one other common explanation of what has happened.

You connected to a web page whose URL has been changed. A page at the old URL automatically redirects you to the page's new location. It may have redirected you so quickly that you did not even notice. If you then click 'back', you will get the redirect page which automatically sends you back to the document you tried to go back from. Use the history list to jump back over the redirect page.

Parasite frames

Webmasters who use frames on their site can force your browser to put their frame on every document you connect to via their site. Thus, 'sinister enterprises' could provide a page of links to a thousand other websites. When you click on those links, whether they be to the United Nations, the Government of India or the Swedish army, those sites will appear within the 'sinister enterprises' frame. Novice users get the impression that 'sinister enterprises' has responsibility for all of these sites. The parasite frame will attach itself to every site you visit during this session.

Escape by returning to the page on the parasite site where you first chose a link to another page. Click on the link you want to go to, hold down the right mouse button and choose 'Open link in new window'. The link will open in a new window free of the parasite frame (Pfaffenberger, 1997: 107).

Understanding error messages

Error 400: Bad request

There is usually a typing error in the URL you have typed in or in the hyperlink you clicked on.

Error 401: Unauthorized

This is often a password-protected page that you can only access if you have registered for the service it is part of.

Error 403: Forbidden

This is usually a page restricted to certain users. For example, a university server might only allow connections from computers in its own domain. No password is required. You will just be refused access if your computer does not have the right IP address.

Error 404: Not found

You have connected successfully to the server but the particular page you requested does not exist, at least not at the URL you have typed. Either you have made a typing mistake in the last part of the URL (after the domain name) or the page has been moved. If you think it has been moved, have a look at the index page of the folder it is in, or at the folder above it to see if you can find a link to it there. For example, if **www.school.edu/ shapes/squares.html** brings up this error, look at **www.school. edu/shapes** and **www. school.edu** for clues as to where it has gone.

Error 500: Internal server error

There is some problem with the server you are trying to connect to. All you can do is try again.

'Host not found'

Either the domain name is wrong (try typing it again) or your computer cannot connect to your DNS server where it looks up IP addresses for servers. If the latter, it may well be there is a problem with your Internet connection.

'Too many connections'

The site you are trying to connect to is overloaded with requests. Try again immediately. If that does not work try again later.

Exercises

Exercise 1: Building a search query

Devise a very specific search query on an aspect of your topic. The query must include at least one exact phrase and one minus sign (or NOT, the Boolean equivalent). You should build this query up gradually, adding new elements in the light of the initial search results. The query in its final form should retrieve no fewer than three results on Google, Bing or Yahoo, of which at least three of the first ten are directly relevant to the topic you're investigating.

For each stage of building the query, briefly describe the following:

1 Your reasons for choosing the elements in the query.
2 The number of hits retrieved and how many of the first ten are directly relevant.
3 The nature of the first ten hits.
4 The way in which you use the information in the first ten hits to refine your search further.

Exercise 2: Restricting by date and site

Taking the search query developed in Exercise 1, or a similarly precise query:

1 Restrict the query to pages updated in the past three months. What difference does this make to the results? How useful is it?

2 Restrict the query to pages from US university sites (edu). What difference does this make to the results? How useful is it?
3 Exclude pages from commercial sites (com). What difference does this make to the results? How useful is it?

Exercise 3: Comparing the three big search engines

Run the search query developed in Exercise 1, or a similarly precise query on the following search engines:

- Google
- Yahoo
- Bing

1 How much overlap is there between the top ten results in each?
2 Compare the relevance of the top five results. Which search engine returns the most relevant results in the top five?
3 Which of the search engines turned up the single most important result?

Exercise 4: Searching by link

Identify a key web page directly related to your topic.

1 Search for links to this page and search for the title of this page as an exact phrase. Compare the results of these two searches.
2 Which is more effective in identifying other web pages that make reference to this key web page?

Exercise 5: Searching by title and URL

Use two or three terms associated with your topic to search for:

- web pages whose title contains any of these terms; and
- web pages whose URL contains any of these terms.

Compare the results of these two searches and briefly describe the advantages and disadvantages of searching by title and URL.

SIX

Social media, news and multimedia

Social media

Web 2.0, Web 3.0 and user-generated content

A famous US court judgment rejecting censorship in the 1990s described the Internet as a 'never-ending world-wide conversation'. This description emphasizes the interactive aspects of the new technologies. Interaction was at the heart of the vision of those who established the Internet and at the heart of the technology in the initial years when email discussion lists, distribution lists and electronic bulletin boards dominated the online world. This initial interactive phase of the Internet was succeeded by a more commercialized top-down Internet dominated by the web pages of existing corporations, institutions and governments. During the past few years, however, the development and spread of a range of new technologies, chief among them blogs and social networks, has brought interaction back to the centre. The Internet may be used as a way to distribute documents and images more quickly and cheaply than before, but the interactive capacities of the Internet are its most distinctive feature as a medium of communication and they are central to fundamental transformations in the way in which we seek and organize information.

In the mid-1990s veteran online researcher Reva Basch conducted interviews with dozens of people who made their living from finding information online (Basch, 1996). Time and again these experienced researchers mentioned in their interviews that the most valuable resource on the Internet was not the big data bases but other human beings. Many of the researchers had stories of how a far-away expert in one particular field was able to answer their question more quickly than they could ever have hoped to have answered it by searching the web or the online databases.

Interaction was initially separated out from the rest of the Internet and took place in newsgroups and on email lists. Blogs (Web logs, to give them their official title) then made it easier for readers to add comments to web pages and played a central role in breaking down the distinction between websites and online interaction. Blogs heralded fundamental changes in the nature of the Internet, making it a far more interactive environment. The emergence of social networking sites such as Bebo (**bebo.com**), MySpace (**myspace.com**), which subsequently gave way to Facebook (**facebook.com**) and Google+ (**plus.google.com**), have made it a simple matter for anyone with Internet access to effectively set up their own complex website and to use it as a focus for interaction with others. These developments have been paralleled by the development of a wide range of new tools that seek to bottle the magic of interaction, to capture the value generated by contact between people.

Web 2.0 is used as shorthand to describe a new generation of online services that, among other things, integrate writer and reader, producer and consumer and blur the boundary between both. Web 3.0 has been used to differentiate between those initial developments and the quantum leap forward that is represented by the spread of social networking and the increasing integration of these new services. The impact of user-generated content stretches far beyond the bounds of social networking sites and can be seen clearly in operation on the Amazon websites, where reader reviews and recommendations now constitute a major component of the service and a powerful research resource for anyone who uses Amazon. 'Conversation is content', as the slogan puts it. Print and broadcast media have also begun to use reader comments as an important part of their content, while even some academic journals have taken an interactive turn, facilitating online discussion and commentary on individual articles they publish.

Figure 6.1   Facebook image

Figure 6.2   Google Plus image

Making the most of online interaction

One of the greatest strengths of social networks, blogs and email discussion lists is that they connect you to people who may be able to quickly answer specialized queries that it would take a lot of work to answer in any other way. They need to be used carefully, however. If you don't ask the right question in the right place, you are likely to be met with silence, or abuse. The advice that follows draws in part on 'The art of getting help' by Phil Agre (1996). The first thing to do is to make sure you are in the right place, that is, on a blog, a group or a list where people will take your query seriously, consider it appropriate and be in a good position to answer it.

Social network groups or discussion lists in your subject area can provide a good forum for initial research queries in a specialized area. This does not mean asking questions like 'please tell me everything you know about the German economy', but rather asking questions about the most useful books on your topic or asking whether there are less obvious sources you should be using. If you ask a question that you could easily answer yourself by checking one or two basic sources, you are unlikely to be received sympathetically. The response to new users asking basic questions online is summed up in the terse abbreviated answer, RTM (Read The Manual), or the less polite RTFM. A lot of websites, blogs and groups have an FAQ (Frequently Asked Questions), a document that can often run to 50 pages in length and that answers the questions most commonly asked on that blog or list.

Blogs, discussion groups and email lists also provide an ideal forum for very specialized research queries. Finally, give something back. The more you contribute to helping others, the more likely it is that others in a group or on a list will be prepared to help when you have a query.

Netiquette

Netiquette refers to a set of informal guidelines for avoiding confrontation in online interaction. It can be very easy to alienate people online. Email, social networks and the web allow instantaneous responses of the kind previously only possible in conversation, where tone and inflection provided a wealth of extra information about the meaning of what was said. Email messages and posts to blogs and social networks are often composed carelessly and hastily by the sender and can be misinterpreted by the recipient. Before you send an email or post a comment on a website or a blog, think twice. Never send a message without re-reading it at least once to check content and spelling. Sometimes you will be amazed to read the things you have typed in haste. Think of the tone too. It is easy to sound abrupt and unfriendly online and it is important to keep to a polite tone with people you do not know. Sarcasm and irony travel notoriously badly via email. Avoid them. And don't type in capitals – people think you're shouting at them. In contributing to online discussion, be aware that messages you write now may be available online for decades afterwards.

Flames, trolls and pigs

Wendy Grossman, one of the first journalists to write extensively on online interaction, compared the Internet to the Babel Fish described by Douglas Adams in *The Hitchhiker's Guide to the Galaxy* (1979). This was a tiny fish you could stick in your ear that would instantly translate any language for you. Adams wrote that the Babel Fish, 'by effectively removing all barriers to communication between different races and cultures, has caused more and bloodier wars than anything else in the history of creation' (cited in Grossman, 1997: 195). The flame wars which rage on social networks, blogs and discussion groups illustrate perfectly the point that easy communication is as likely to facilitate conflict as cooperation.

Flames are abusive email messages. Flame wars often begin with disagreement in an email discussion that escalates rapidly into mutual abuse, fits of screaming, threats of violence and finally a full-scale flame war that drags other people into the conflict.

Fascinated by flames in much the same way that arsonists are, many people deliberately try to provoke conflict. For some it is a form of recreation to post messages that are so provocative, so filled with hate and invective or so obtuse that other subscribers get whipped up into a frenzy. Those who post these messages just to see what reaction they provoke are called 'trolls'. Just ignore them. 'Never wrestle with a pig. You both get dirty, and the pig likes it,' as one Net saying puts it (Grossman, 1997: 108).

Blogs

One of the defining features of a blog is that it allows readers to add comments to individual posts. The comments then become an integral part of the blog. Many blogs are used as personal diaries, infrequently updated and of little interest to those beyond an immediate circle of family and friends. At the other end of the spectrum are elaborate blogs maintained jointly by several individuals, often involving organizations, and acting as a major central resource in the area with which they are concerned. Some of the most prominent and respected social scientists and humanities scholars have blogs through which they sometimes distribute work in progress or working papers and indicate their current interests.

Bloggers link intensively to other blogs through a 'blogroll'. If you find one good blog in your area it will lead you to others.

Blogs are structured in a way that makes it easy to make regular new additions. Content is constantly displaced and renewed as older material is pushed to the bottom. Partly because bloggers tend to emphasize the current moment, blogs have a high rate of attrition. Bloggers work intently on keeping a blog updated for several months or a few years and then discover they don't have the time to maintain that level of commitment. The blog simply disappears.

One of the most common types of blog is the news blog, focused on current affairs, commenting on news stories in a particular area or from a particular ideological perspective. Many bloggers argue that the distinction between high-quality news blogs and traditional print and broadcast media is now meaningless and that serious bloggers are entitled to the same recognition as print journalists. As newspapers and television stations establish their own blogs, the gap between traditional and new media is narrowing rapidly. Traditional media argue, on the other hand, that bloggers are almost entirely dependent on print and broadcast media for the stories on which they comment.

Many blogs focus intently on current events or current developments in a particular specialized academic field, and act as excellent guides to new resources in those fields. They can usefully supplement a good subject guide in the area by providing a way to keep up to date with new developments. You can sign up to RSS feeds to keep in touch with new entries.

Although this is not inherent to the software or to blogging as a practice, a large proportion of blogs are devoted to highlighting and commenting on stories that have appeared elsewhere, in both traditional media and other blogs. As a result, a single and often very specific story in a newspaper or blog or on a TV or radio station can be the subject of comment in thousands of blogs. Each of these blog entries can attract comments in turn from several readers of the blog in question. While many blog entries and much of the comment on those blogs add little to an understanding of the issues covered in stories, some of the comment adds important additional material and perspectives unavailable elsewhere. If your research involves an issue of contemporary controversy, this provides a genuinely novel kind of resource for detailed investigation of the minute detail of very specific issues.

Searching blogs

The major keyword search engines pick up blogs in their searches but there are also a number of specialized services for searching blogs. Their main advantage is that they exclude everything but the blogs. Blogs as a genre are much more clearly structured than web pages in general. While it can be difficult to identify what site a web page belongs to, it's simple to identify what blog a post belongs to. Search results in the blog search engines include both the titles of individual messages and of the blog they were posted to. This makes it easy to identify the wider context a post is located in. Bloggers add descriptive tags to individual posts and to their blogs, providing a set of subject keywords for almost every item in the blogosphere.

All of this should make it easy to search for useful, relevant blogs, but it doesn't. The bulk of blogs do not confine themselves to a single subject but deal with a wide range of topics the author is interested in. It's common for two or three different subjects to come up in passing in a single post. In the circumstances, searching by subject can be one of the least productive ways to approach the blogosphere.

Blogs are concerned above all with the current moment, in the same way as newspapers and television news. Bloggers sweep one way and then the other as public debates shift direction. One of the most productive ways to use blogs is to go with this flow, to use the blogs to trace comment on very specific events and debates, organizing your search around key news stories rather than around subject areas. The scale of public debate is so overwhelming that you can only realistically consider tracing a very specific debate. It would be a lifetime's work to trace, for example, any one of the major themes in public debates associated with the September 11 attacks in the USA. It is much more realistic to take a story like the 2005 article in the science journal *Nature* which argued that Wikipedia was not much more inaccurate than *Encyclopaedia Britannica* (Giles, 2005), a claim strongly contested by the latter (*Encyclopaedia Britannica*, 2006). A search on **Encyclopaedia Britannica Wikipedia** brings up several hundred results in the blog search engine Technorati. Many of them were not relevant to this particular story, but limiting the search to blogs with 'a lot of authority' reduced the number to 23. One effect of this restriction was to cut out a lot of private blogs and to bring to the top blogs that enjoy a lot of links precisely because they are a focus for public debate. Virtually all of the hits in this restricted search make direct reference to this story and lead you to the key newspaper and magazine articles that deal with the issue.

Google Blog Search (**blogsearch.google.com**) Google Blog Search sorts results by relevance. The advanced search allows you to limit your search to the titles of blogs, to an individual blog, or to posts written by a particular individual. You can also restrict your search very tightly by date.

Technorati (**www.technorati.com**) Technorati has a number of unique features that take advantage of the clearly structured character of blogs. Search results allow you to connect directly to individual posts or to the home page of the blog they belong to. 'Click to refine this search' provides you with additional search options. You can filter your search by topic, limiting it to 'politics' or 'technology', for example. You can order results by date (bringing the most recent posts to the top) or by 'authority', bringing the most-linked-to blogs and posts to the top.

Figure 6.3 Technorati image

Sorting by 'authority' can provide a very effective way to exclude personal blogs and to confine your search to blogs which are part of a vibrant wider network and which are more likely to be a site of public debate and interchange. Search 'blogs' (as opposed to posts) using broad search terms that describe your subject to identify the most popular blogs in your area. Technorati displays the number of 'incoming links' to a blog in the search results, indicating how many other blogs link to them. Technorati provides a regularly updated list of the hundred most popular blogs (**technorati.com/blogs/top100**), a list dominated by current affairs and technology blogs.

BlogPulse (**www.blogpulse.com**) BlogPulse allows you to search blogs and to generate lists of blogs that link to the blog you are interested in. You can also chart blog 'trends', identifying changes over time in the frequency with which your search terms are mentioned in the blogosphere, and identifying the most popular search terms.

Social networks

The private lives of millions of people have exploded into the public realm with dramatic consequences, generating an abrupt increase in the number of people online and in the intensity and regularity of online interaction. The initial focus of most social networks was private lives and personal networks, but it wasn't long before universities, research institutes, non-governmental organizations, campaign groups, traditional media outlets, political parties and corporations realized the importance of having a presence on these networks. As a consequence, the boundary between the 'personal', the professional, the political and the public is increasingly blurred on these networks and they constitute a major site of public discussion and academic interchange.

The limitations of social networking sites that were primarily dominated by the personal helped to generate the establishment of social networks that were solely dedicated to academic research and academic networking, such as **academia.edu** and **CiteULike**. They are dealt with in Chapter 9. But even the networks which are targeted primarily at the personal inevitably become a forum for the discussion of current issues. If you are interested in public debate on a very specific topic and are doing a 'needle in the haystack' search, it may be worth doing a search of these sites. In several social networks you can only use the search facilities within the network if you have signed up. However, you can search all of them through the major search engines. Add **site:facebook.com** or **site:plus.google.com** to your query to limit the search to these sites. Users of these sites may hide their pages from public view and no search will allow you to search the full contents of these sites. The Facebook search box does a combined search that includes people, pages and groups as well as posts to Facebook and Facebook groups, but it doesn't appear to search the full text of all of these. You can limit your search to any one of these categories. It also does a limited search of the web with Bing for some reason, bringing back a few key results.

Openbook (**openbook.org**) searches Facebook updates, primarily as a means of alerting people to the fact that some very personal material posted to Facebook can be searched and retrieved by anyone.

Kurrently (**kurrently.com**), a 'real-time search engine for Twitter and Facebook', finds recent posts containing your search term and updates the screen continuously. You can limit the search to one or other of the two services.

The social media section in *Mashable.com* (**mashable.com/social-media/**) provides regular news on the latest developments in social networking services.

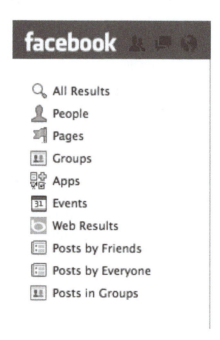

Figure 6.4   Search options in Facebook

Figure 6.5 Twitter search image

Twitter (Twitter.com)

'Following' some of the key people or centres in your area provides a way to stay a little bit ahead of the curve. It also provides you with direct access of a kind to people who might otherwise be inaccessible. Many researchers and prominent academics use Twitter to distribute information about papers they have just published or upcoming events they are involved in or working papers or drafts that they have made available online. Key institutions, research institutes and academic programmes also tweet, in many cases to point you to new materials available online. Search the full text of tweets, and choose people to follow, at **twitter.com**

Wikis

Wikis take interaction one step further than the blogs. A Wiki is a website that allows multiple viewers to easily edit its contents. The resulting website is the product of a collaborative effort sometimes involving thousands of people improving, correcting and adding. At its worst, it involves viewers deliberately including false information in pursuit of their own agenda, as in the case of the political staffers in the USA, who were briefly banned from Wikipedia after it was found that they were adding misleading information about the politicians they worked for and their opponents (Wikinews, 2006).

Wikipedia (**www.wikipedia.org**) is the best known Wiki project (see Chapter 2), but there are also large numbers of specialized Wikis, many of them aimed at building up resources and knowledge-sharing in specific academic subject areas. To limit your search to Wikis in the big search engines, try adding **wiki** or **inurl:wiki** to your search query. Wiki is increasingly being included in the domain names and URLs of Wikis, making the **inurl** search quite effective. A good Wiki in your area can act as a kind of collaborative subject guide, and can be much more detailed than anything produced by a single individual or organization could be.

Email lists

Mailing lists continue to serve a certain purpose, although many of their functions have been taken over by blogs and social networks in recent years. There are now far fewer discussion lists than there used to be. Distribution lists are used to send materials in one direction only, like the lists that publishers use to send out regular updates on their new publications, and these remain important. Discussion lists are quite different, acting as forums for exchange and debate. Many discussion lists are unmoderated. The list owner plays no role in channelling or directing the discussion that takes place. These lists tend to get rapidly bogged down in flame wars and are of limited use. Moderated lists are lists in which a list moderator, a real human being, plays some role in filtering or editing messages posted to the list. Most moderators do not use a heavy hand, merely stopping abusive and irrelevant email from being posted to the list. Perhaps the most useful lists are those that are very heavily moderated, such as the suite of academic discussion lists under the authority of H-Net (see below).

There are likely to be at least one or two academic email lists dealing with your subject area that it would be useful to subscribe to. There are a few search engines devoted to searching the titles and short descriptions of email lists, but these will turn up a bewildering array of results. It's far quicker to identify email lists by other routes. Ask other people working in the area what lists they use. Check subject guides in your area (see Chapter 4). They usually include the best known and most active lists. Check the websites of the key professional associations concerned with your subject to see if they provide discussion lists. Check too to see if there is an H-Net or JISCmail list in your subject area.

H-Net: Humanities and Social Sciences Online (**www.h-net.org**) H-Net was initially concerned only with history but has broadened out to deal with the humanities in general and with certain areas in the social sciences too. The H-Net lists are one of the most valuable academic resources on the Internet. Each H-Net list has an editor and an editorial board and is controlled almost as tightly as a print publication. Membership of the lists is composed of academics, postgraduate students and other interested groups, such as journalists and librarians. Editors actively contribute to the lists themselves, powering them along and ensuring that the lists never die from inactivity. Even if you don't join an H-Net list, you can access the H-Net website and the sites for individual H-Net lists and search their archives. If you find the right list, the archives can provide a very focused collection of high-quality material in your subject area. Many of the lists have a very strong US emphasis.

JISCMAIL (**www.jiscmail.ac.uk**) This is a collection of thousands of lists serving the academic community in the UK, many of them very specialized and catering to particular research groups. You can search by keyword for lists of interest to you. You can also restrict this keyword search to lists in a particular subject area, such as the humanities. Alternatively, you can browse the full list of lists. The keyword search does not search the full text of list archives but only the titles and descriptions of lists.

Lurking

The vast majority of list members never contribute anything to a list, not a single question or answer, let alone an eloquent contribution to debate. One survey of list users showed that 83 per cent of them had never contributed anything. Only about 6 per cent had sent more than one or two messages (Kitchin, 1998: 83, citing Kawakami). The typical list subscriber is a 'lurker' who reads but does not contribute.

Mailing list search engines

Search engines which search only for lists do not provide the best way to identify key lists in your area, but once you have identified the key lists in your area by other means you can check these search engines to see if you have missed out on any major lists. Look for lists with large numbers of subscribers. Descriptions of lists can sometimes be inaccurate or too short to be informative.

> *CataList, the official catalog of LISTSERV lists* (**www.lsoft.com/catalist.html**) This only includes lists that use the LISTSERV software. It covers more than 50,000 public lists. It responds best to simple searching, the broadest terms and every variation on those terms. If it is Scottish matters you are interested in, for example, be sure to search for Scot, Scots, Scotland, Scottish and any other variation you can think of. Each will bring up a different set of results. A huge proportion of lists use this software and CataList provides the best searchable database of these particular lists, one that, according to them, is kept constantly updated. It searches the titles and short descriptions of lists and you can arrange lists by the number of subscribers they have. It also tells you if lists are archived on the web. It seems only a small minority are.

Lists to avoid

Avoid lists that are dead or dying. Since only a tiny proportion of list subscribers ever contribute, it stands to reason that a list with fewer than 100 subscribers is likely to have very little traffic. Constantly active discussion lists, by contrast, will generally have over 1,000 subscribers and you will usually discover that there are quite a limited number of such discussion lists in your area of interest. Avoid private lists too. These are lists set up by an organization or group of individuals connected by work or a cooperative venture of some kind. Membership is restricted to those at the organization concerned or actively involved in the venture. They were never intended to be publicized at all.

Discussion groups

Discussion groups have faded in popularity as social networks have expanded and taken over many of their functions but they remain important in certain areas. In addition, deep archives have been built up over the years and searching these archives turns up material that you won't get through a search of the open Web. Messages to discussion groups are posted to the groups online. As a result, messages are archived and easily searchable, unlike the messages in email discussion lists.

As with email messages, the best search strategy is to identify one or two key groups directly relevant to your interests. You can do this by searching the titles and short descriptions of groups using very broad search terms. Alternatively, you can search the discussion group archives to locate references to very specific terms in individual messages.

When searching discussion groups, be aware that these posts are much more casual items than web pages or even blogs. They are often written in haste, words are frequently misspelled, abbreviations are used and language is often very casual. This has an impact on the kind of search terms that are most useful.

It is a simple matter for anyone with Internet access to set up a group of their own in either Google Groups or Yahoo Groups.

Google Groups (**groups.google.com**) Google Groups began when Google took over the running of the Usenet Newsgroups, one of the oldest forums for online interaction. The Usenet archives available through Google Groups include over a billion messages and date back to 1981. Many non-Usenet groups have subsequently been added to Google Groups.

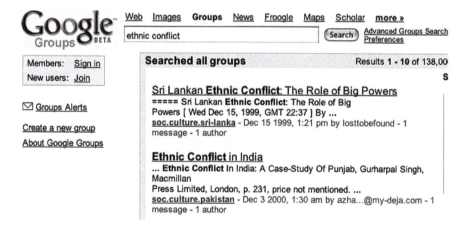

Figure 6.6   Google Groups search results on ethnic conflict

To limit your search to the titles and descriptions of groups, 'Search for a group'. You can also browse through groups organized by subject category. All of the groups returned in the search results are grouped according to topic, 'messages per month' and number of members, as well as language, making it a simple matter to identify the largest groups in your subject area. You can limit your searches to individual topics when you search the full text of posts.

When you do an ordinary search in Google Groups, searching the full text of posts, the results list will be headed by groups that match your search term. The other results show a group name, a brief description of the group and the date of the last post. These dates provide an indication of the declining popularity of groups and the relatively small proportion of recent posts. The results also provide links to a full list of discussions in groups that include your search term. These discussions consist of all of the individual messages that belonged to a particular discussion.

In the advanced search, you can limit the search by author, allowing you to trace the posts of an individual contributor. This emphasizes that when you post messages to discussion groups you are laying out a trail of opinions which can be easily followed by others years later. You can also limit your search very tightly by date. If you are interested in a particular event, this allows you to focus on the interaction that took place immediately after the event.

Usenet hierarchies in Google Groups

Usenet Newsgroups had their own system of hierarchical ordering according to subject category before they came under Google's wing. Subsequently, thousands of additional groups have been added to Google Groups but have not been slotted into the Usenet hierarchies. Instead, Google has created a new system of categorizing groups by subject. A huge proportion of the Google groups are still part of that Usenet hierarchy, however, and understanding it can help you to identify relevant groups.

Below is a list of some of the top-level Usenet hierarchies relevant to the social sciences and humanities:

- Alt – alternative
- Comp – computers
- Misc – miscellaneous
- Rec – recreation and hobbies
- Sci – science
- Soc – society, culture, religion
- Talk – discussion, focused on current issues

(Continued)

(Continued)

Each of these is home to hundreds or even thousands of individual newsgroups. The top level of the hierarchy is the first part of a newsgroup name. For example, **soc. culture** belongs to the soc hierarchy. It is for discussion of culture in general. **soc.culture.indian** also belongs to the soc hierarchy and is for the discussion of Indian culture. **soc.culture. indian.kerala** is for discussion of the culture of the Indian state of Kerala. There are also top-level hierarchies specific to certain regions, including **de** (Germany), **au** (Australia) and **uk** (United Kingdom), that provide groups which will be of interest to users dealing with these particular areas or countries.

Yahoo Groups (**groups.yahoo.com**) Yahoo Groups are organized into subject categories. When you search in Yahoo Groups, you search the titles of subject categories, and the titles and long descriptions of the groups. You do not search the full text of messages. You can also browse by subject. The subject categories are not particularly useful because a broad category, such as Geography, includes huge numbers of local groups targeted at a particular research group or a particular set of students, for example. These groups are of minimal value to a wider audience and they dominate the results in some categories. Search results show you how many members each group has but it is not as easy to limit your search to larger groups as it is in Google Groups.

News

Current news is available in big spadefuls all across the web, searchable by keyword and by topic. The big online news services, such as Yahoo News (**news.yahoo. com**), Google News (**news.google.com**) and MSNBC (**www.msnbc.msn.com**), draw on a wide variety of newspapers, TV and radio stations and wire news services for their content. They include audio, video and text. Google News, for example, draws on over 4,500 news sources. There is a huge overlap in the coverage of these big services. Google News services are tailored to audiences in different countries.

The advanced search options of both Yahoo News and Google News allow you to restrict your search to individual news sources, to particular countries or regions or to stories by a particular journalist or author. You can restrict your search very tightly by date. Yahoo News also allows you to limit your search to broad subject categories, such as politics or health. All of the services are extremely shallow in terms of time. To get deeper historical coverage you need to go to the news archive databases. Google News and Yahoo News allow you to limit your search to news stories from the previous hour or day or week or month.

RSS: Really Simple Syndication

RSS provides a popular way of keeping up with news without having to regularly return to the relevant web pages. An RSS feed provides you with short summaries of the stories currently available at a particular web page and links directly to the stories themselves. RSS readers make it easier to organize information from all of the sites you return to regularly. RSS and Atom are two of the most common formats for delivering such feeds. Browsers such as Firefox now make it a simple matter to bookmark an RSS feed by clicking the RSS symbol to the right of the URL at the top of the browser. Add the feed to your bookmarks toolbar for easy regular access.

LexisNexis (**www.lexisnexis.com**) LexisNexis provides the full text of articles from thousands of newspapers. You can restrict searches to publications from particular countries or to individual publications. A 'source directory' lists the different publications that are available. Partly because they have been in the online database business for so long, LexisNexis has the deepest historical coverage of several major British and American newspapers. It is only available if your university or library subscribes to the service.

News Library (**www.newslibrary.com**) This is an archive of articles from more than 800 newspapers, heavily weighted to US material and including large numbers of local and regional newspapers in the USA. Coverage in terms of time varies greatly from one newspaper to the other. Flexible search options allow you to search one or all or any combination of newspaper titles in the archive. Anyone can search for free and retrieve the first paragraph of an article but if you want to see the full text you have to pay. It also searches transcripts of television and radio programmes and the archives of some wire services. The advanced search allows you to limit your search to headlines or to the first paragraph of a story. The first paragraph usually distils the content of the entire article ('Who's gonna read the second paragraph?', as the editor said to the reporter in *The Front Page*, a classic 1931 film about the newspaper business).

ProQuest News & Magazines is one of the databases provided by ProQuest, which also produces databases of academic articles. If your institution is a subscriber, there should be a link from your library's website. It covers over 1,400 newspapers and magazines. Records for most papers go back no further than 1986 but this gives the database a greater historical depth than some others. Information from the larger newspapers can be on the database within 24 hours of publication.

The bulk of newspapers and magazines have websites that provide access to their own archives. In some cases they simply provide another route to the archives held in the databases listed above. The archives of individual newspapers can in some cases be more complete and are searchable in very different ways from the articles from those papers which form part of larger databases. It can sometimes be difficult to find your way to the archive of a newspaper from its website. Because of the focus on the present moment, archives are often buried deep within the websites and you may need to do a little digging to find them.

The sites listed below maintain large collections of links to the websites of individual newspapers, magazines and broadcast media.

- *Internet Public Library List of Newspapers* (**www.ipl.org/div/news**) Links are organized geographically and are searchable by keyword.
- *Newslink* (**www.newslink.org**) Links to newspapers, magazines and broadcast media.
- *Yahoo: News and Media Category* (**www.dir.yahoo.com/News_and_Media/**) This guide links to a huge variety of news sites, organized by media type, by subject, and by country.
- *Wikipedia: Lists of newspapers* (**en.wikipedia.org/wiki/Lists_of_newspapers**) provides a geographically organized list of links to Wikipedia entries for newspapers all over the world. The national lists tend to be comprehensive and also include newspapers that are now defunct. They provide links to the websites of newspapers if such websites exist.

These listings usually make little attempt to distinguish between newspapers of record, which emphasize accuracy and the ideal of objective reporting, and newspapers which place less emphasis on these ideals. If you are looking for newspapers from a particular country, a better starting point can often be a general web guide to resources on that country, which will almost always include annotated links to that country's media. Many newspapers charge fees for full access to their archives, although you can often conduct searches and read extracts from articles for free.

Wire services

Wire services, such as AFP, PA and UPI, have become a principal source of news information on the web because even before its advent they were geared up to rapid and flexible worldwide delivery of news. Most newspapers have taken stories from these services for decades, using them for coverage of countries where they themselves could not afford to have a full-time reporter. Now the wire news feed which once came into the offices of newspapers is available to anyone through the web, and the wire services have made deals to provide searchable up-to-date news via almost every search engine, portal and news site on the Internet. Below is a list of some of the major wire services.

- *AFP: Agence France Press*, France (**www.afp.com**)
- *AP: The Associated Press*, US (**www.ap.org**) You can search news from the previous seven days, including photos, video and audio. You can search the archive for free and buy the full text of articles going back to 1998 (**www.newslibrary.com/sites/apab**).
- *China View: Xinhua online*, the Chinese government news agency (**www.chinaview.cn**)
- *PA: Press Association*, UK (**www.pressassociation.co.uk**) This service is aimed primarily at serving journalists and the media.
- *Reuters*, UK (**today.reuters.com/news/**)
- *TASS*, Russia (**www.itar-tass.com/en**)
- *UPI: United Press International*, US (**www.upi.com**)

You will find news reports all over the Internet, placed by individuals on their websites, blogs or social networks or forwarded by email. Beware of second-hand news items. Always try to find the original version. It is a simple matter for someone to crop or alter a text to suit their own purposes before they forward it or put it on the web.

Multimedia

Visual and audio resources have not been heavily used in research in many social science and humanities disciplines. One reason for this was the inaccessibility of these resources and the lack of specialized technical knowledge. The Internet has made it a much simpler matter to locate and to manipulate images and sound. Some of the biggest broadcasters have begun to experiment with making a wide range of film clips, audio clips and images available for free under a variety of 'creative commons' licences, which allow people to use these copyright materials under certain conditions. One of the leaders in this is Britain's *BBC* (**www.bbc.co.uk**). Materials are often made available on condition that the original author is acknowledged and that they are not used for commercial purposes. It is now a much simpler matter for a research student to use video and audio clips as well as a wide range of images in a thesis or dissertation.

In addition, there has been a dramatic increase in the multimedia resources made available through social networks and other Web 2.0 or Web 3.0 services. Among the most popular things for people to share and publicize through these sites are the videos, images and sounds they themselves have produced. In some cases, these services have effectively become massive new public libraries full of multimedia resources, many of which can be used by anyone.

Many web pages and websites incorporate a wide range of media, mixing video clips with images and animated graphics, and there is no clear boundary between print and audio and visual resources online. However, there are a number of services devoted specifically to locating non-text resources.

Images

Image searches are available in Google, Yahoo and Bing. Because images are often accompanied by very little text, you need to use broad search terms rather than the very specific queries you use to search the full text of documents. Because images are often not clearly labelled, you may need to try a variety of search terms related to your topic. If a keyword search turns up one image relevant to your search, you can go to the web page where the image is imbedded to see if it is part of a wider collection of related images.

Photo sharing websites provide an additional source of images online. Several such sites, including *Photobucket* (**photobucket.com**), *Flickr* (**www.flickr.com**), *Picasa* (**picasaweb.google.com**) and *PBase* (**pbase.com**), contain millions of photographs posted by individual users. Many of the photographs on these sites are restricted to certain viewers while many others are available for a fee, but a huge proportion of the photographs are freely available to anyone. If you use photographs from these sites, you need to credit photographers and ensure that you are entitled to use the photos. These collections do not overlap to any great degree. If you are searching for a very specific image it is well worth searching all of them.

One of the best known of these sites is Flickr (**www.flickr.com**). Flickr provides an illustration of several features that are common to many of these sites. Individual photographers add descriptive tags (keywords) and sometimes short descriptions to their photographs. The advanced search (**www.flickr.com/search/advanced**) allows you to search for one or more tags or to simultaneously search titles, tags and descriptions of the photographs. It also allows you to limit your search to specific time periods.

Results are organized into tag clusters that group pictures according to the broad themes suggested by the other tags used to describe them. This can very effectively sort the results by theme and can also suggest related tags that it might be useful to search on. You can use individual photographs to guide you to relevant collections by exploring the collections of the photographer. In addition, Flickr users have created groups (collections based on a common theme), to which large numbers of people can post their images. Individual images can lead you to groups of related images and you can sign up for regular updates on new additions to these groups.

There are also large numbers of commercial image banks and stock photography services that allow users to search massive collections of images, some of them royalty-free, others for sale. You will find a wide range of these services by searching a search engine for **"image bank"** or **"stock photography"**.

One major source of images online remains inaccessible to the general public. Some of the biggest media companies which sell images to newspapers, magazines and design professionals still don't make these huge image banks easily and cheaply available to the general public.

Search strategy

Searching for images

Flickr is particularly strong on contemporary images and a search for historical photographs of the Berlin Wall on Flickr yields relatively little. **Berlin Wall** returns recent photos of the pieces of wall that remain, but relatively few historical photographs. However, clicking on just one of these historical images brings up a text that includes links to a collection of historical Berlin Wall photographs. In addition, the search results also provide a link to a 'Berlin wall' group with more than 1,000 members and more than 6,000 photographs. Limiting your search to this group, you can call up historical photographs by using search terms associated with the time when the wall still existed, such as 'grenzpolizei' (border police) or '1961' (the year of the wall's construction) or indeed any year from the period when the wall existed, given that so many people add the year to their historical photographs. The Berlin Wall came down in 1989 and a search on **Berlin Wall 1989** retrieves hundreds of photographs portraying the fall of the wall. By contrast, a search in Google Images on **Berlin Wall history** brings back millions of results. Because there are so many results, the search can be narrowed very precisely and a search on **Berlin Wall Grenzpolizei** turns up hundreds of images of the East German border police and of the wall and the border before reunification.

The Yahoo Images search returns over 20,000 results for **Berlin Wall history** and points you to several collections of historical photos that didn't turn up in the first few screens of the Google search. By this stage the search has identified several useful collections.

These image search engines do not necessarily provide the only way or the best way to identify collections of images. If you do your image searching using the ordinary search engines, you can be much more specific than you can when using the image search facilities. A search in Google or Bing or Yahoo on **Berlin Wall photographs historical archive** brings up several links to websites providing historical photographic archives of the Berlin Wall.

Maps

Images of maps from a wide range of sources are available on the image search engines listed above and on the photo sharing sites. Adding **map** to your query will narrow your search very effectively in all of these services. You will often find that the same map is available online at many different locations. In these cases you need to track down the original source in order to find out which organization or individual produced the map and to credit them accordingly.

One of the largest online map collections is the *Perry-Castañeda Library Map Collection* (**www.lib.utexas.edu/maps**). It also provides a guide to other map sources online. There are many blogs devoted to online maps. One of the most prominent is *The Map Room: A Weblog About Maps* (**maproomblog.com**).

More recently, *Google Maps* (**maps.google.com**) and *Yahoo Maps* (**maps.yahoo.com**) have begun to open up a wide range of new possibilities for online maps. Large numbers of individual users have begun to create their own specialized maps to display data such as crime figures or property prices using Google maps. These are referred to as mashups. Several blogs are devoted to covering the latest developments in Google maps and online mapping in general, among them *Google Maps Mania* (**googlemapsmania.blogspot.com**).

Video

Over the past few years, many millions of individuals have put their own video footage online, using new technologies for videocasting (video podcasting) and vlogging (video blogging) as well as posting to sites like YouTube. In addition, television stations, academic institutions and a wide variety of commercial and non-profit organizations have begun to make video materials, and video archives much more freely available online. As broadcasters begin to make mainstream television programmes available online for free or at a minimal charge, the distinction between television and the Internet is being steadily eroded.

Because programmes that have been broadcast on television include 'closed captions', you can search the full text of these broadcasts, if they are available online. Note that closed captioning is not always completely accurate. For video that hasn't been broadcast, you are limited to searching titles and the short descriptions or keywords provided by those who produced them.

The Moving Image Gateway (MIG) (**www.bufvc.ac.uk/gateway**) is maintained by the British Universities Film and Video Council (BUFVC). It acts as a guide to over 1,000 online resources relevant to the use of audio and video materials at university level. You can browse by subject or search by keyword. The *UCLA Arts Library* provides a guide to 'Selected Internet Sources for Film, Television, Theater' (**www.library.ucla.edu/libraries/arts/9830.cfm**) that includes links to other online guides, film archives and relevant databases.

One rich source of legally-available freely downloadable films is the *Internet Archive's Moving Image Archive* (**www.archive.org/details/movies**). It includes archive documentary films, propaganda films and films that have gone out of copyright.

Academic video resources have also become much more freely available online. *ResearchChannel* (**www.researchchannel.org**), a 'Social Sciences Video and Webcast Library' established by a consortium of US universities and libraries, provides access to video of thousands of academic events and lectures. It is heavily focused on US politics and international politics. It also provides advice on educational use of these materials.

Among the most common genres of video material available online are movie trailers, music videos, personal home video, videos produced by political organizations, video of protests and public events, and archive footage. Some of the search engines also pick up video clips hosted on the websites of television stations. You can do a much more comprehensive search of these stations' output by searching them directly. You can find the websites of most television stations by simply typing the station's name into one of the big keyword search engines.

Among the major video search engines are:

- *Google Video* (**video.google.com**)
- *Yahoo Video Search* (**video.search.yahoo.com**)
- *AOL Video* (**video.aol.com**) (also searches audio materials)

A number of services allow individuals to place their own videos online. Among the better known of these are:

- *YouTube* (**www.youtube.com**)
- *Vimeo* (**www.vimeo.com**)

Video weblogs, or vlogs, are distinguished from the video sources listed above because they are presented as a kind of online TV series in the same way that many podcasts are presented as a kind of regular radio show.

Audio

Many radio stations make audio files of their broadcasts available online, including material from their huge archives of news and documentary programmes. You can also listen online to the current output of a huge proportion of the world's local and national radio stations, over 5,000 of them broadcasting online. You can find most stations easily by searching for the name of the station, and its location if necessary, in one of the keyword search engines.

When you search these sites for audio files you are generally searching short text descriptions of the files and your search terms need to be correspondingly broad. More recently, it has become possible to automatically generate text files from audio files, allowing you to do full-text searches within the content of files. This will allow much more precise searching of audio materials but this technology is still in its infancy.

CADENSA (**cadensa.bl.uk**) is the online catalogue of the British Library National Sound Archive. This extraordinary collection includes recordings of interviews, debates and music, including obscure recordings of former politicians and other prominent political figures. You can search this database of over 2.5 million recordings but you have to visit the Library if you want to listen to them (**www.bl.uk/nsa**). *National Public Radio* in the USA provides a free online archive of thousands of hours of their programmes going back to 1996, including news broadcasts. The search box on the NPR website searches the archives as well as current content (**www.npr.org**).

Podcasting

Podcasting provides an easy way for people to make their own audio recordings available online. The new technology has sparked a rapid increase in the variety and number of audio materials available online. Many of the podcasts have a very experimental and amateur character. If podcasts become significant to people researching your topic, they should begin to feature in subject guides or discussion lists in your area. This might provide a quicker way to identify useful materials than searching the podcast search engines dealt with below.

However, because so many podcasts are ephemeral, the guides may not pick them up. It can also be useful to search for them by searching blog search engines, searching for **podcast** and the appropriate keywords. If a significant interview or statement or resource has been made available by podcast, it may have been picked up by the bloggers who comment on current affairs, even if it never made it into a subject guide.

Some podcasts are modelled on radio shows. A podcast series consists of a number of episodes. You may identify a useful series or a short extract from a particular episode that deals with your topic. Huge numbers of podcasts are locally focused or, like the blogs, deal with an eclectic range of subjects determined by the personal interests of the podcaster.

Apple iTunes: podcasts (**www.apple.com/itunes/podcasts**) You can search and subscribe to podcasts through the Apple iTunes store, which provides sophisticated options for managing podcasts on an iPod.

PodcastAlley (**www.podcastalley.com**) You can search by keyword or browse through lists of podcasts organized by genre.

Podcast Search Service (**www.podcastsearchservice.com**) You can organize search results according to the popularity of the podcasts.

Exercises

Exercise 1: Searching blogs

Identify a specific news story you are interested in. Search in Technorati and in Google Blog Search to find references to this story. If the first news story you identify turns up no search results, try again with a story that is more likely to have generated online debate.

1 When you have developed a query that generates useful results, compare the results on Technorati and Google Blog Search. How much overlap is there between the first five results?
2 Which of them generates the most useful results? Give reasons for your answer.
3 Explore one or two of the related tags generated by these searches that seem likely to be useful.
4 List one or two key print articles identified in your blog search.
5 Use the titles of these articles as search phrases to search again for discussion of the stories. Briefly describe the results and the usefulness of this search.

Exercise 2: Searching email lists

Find the H-Net list most relevant to your research topic. Search the list's archives (if possible) using a few broad terms and a few specific phrases related to your research topic. Try searching using the title of a key book in your area.

1 Briefly describe the results of this search.
2 If it can be done easily, subscribe to the list. Watch the traffic for a few days. Based on this traffic, is the list likely to be useful to you? Explain your answer.
3 Search for a JISCmail list relevant to your research topic by browsing the subject categories, then search for a JISCmail list by keyword. Compare these two methods of identifying a relevant list.
4 Briefly describe the search process by which you identified a relevant JISCmail list.

Exercise 3: Searching discussion groups

1 Use a precise and distinctive query in Google Groups to identify two or three key groups relevant to your topic. Pick one of these groups and search within the group.
2 Describe one or two relevant discussions turned up by your search.
3 How useful are these discussions to you?
4 Use broader search terms in Yahoo Groups to identify two or three key groups relevant to your topic. Do these groups seem likely to be useful?

Exercise 4: Searching for images

1   Identify a type of image that would usefully illustrate your research topic. Search for images of this type using the image search facilities of at least two of the following search engines:

- o Google
- o Yahoo
- o Bing

Use the results to identify collections of related images.

2   Search for images of this type in at least two photo sharing sites, such as:

- o Flickr
- o Webshots
- o Photobucket
- o Pbase

Use the results to identify a photographer or a photo pool that provides related images.

3   Search for images in at least two keyword search engines, such as:

- o Bing
- o Google
- o Yahoo

Use the results to identify collections of related images.

4   Describe the process of developing these search queries in each case.
5   Compare the experience of searching and the search results generated by these different searches.

Exercise 5: Searching for video

Identify a television station likely to provide material relevant to your research. Search and explore the station's website to identify video clips relevant to your research.

1   Briefly describe the video materials this station makes available, the various methods of searching for them and, in your experience, the most successful search approaches to this particular site.
2   Search for video clips relevant to your research in at least two video search engines, such as:

- o Google Video
- o Yahoo Video Search
- o AOL Video

How much overlap was there between the top five results for the most useful search query you devised?

3 What kinds of material did these searches turn up?

4 How do these materials compare with the materials identified by searching the television station?

5 Search for video clips relevant to your research in at least two of the following services or in similar services:

   o YouTube
   o IFILM
   o Vimeo

How much overlap was there between the top five results for the most useful search query you devised.

6 What kinds of material did these searches turn up?

7 How do these materials compare with the materials identified by searching the television station?

Exercise 6: Searching for audio

Identify a radio station likely to provide material relevant to your research. Search and explore the station's website to identify audio clips relevant to your research.

Briefly describe the audio materials this station makes available, the various methods of searching for them and, in your experience, the most successful search approaches to this particular site.

SEVEN

Governments, archives and statistics

Niall Ó Dochartaigh and Patricia Sleeman

Introduction

Government publications, official archives and data collected by government statistical offices are central to much research in the social sciences and humanities. The Internet has dramatically increased the accessibility of these primary sources.

Like the academic articles and books dealt with in earlier chapters, the resources covered in this chapter are clearly marked off from the open Web, and are characterized by well developed and often very complex organizational structures, indexes and classification schemes. To a much greater degree than with any other online resource, it is essential to get to know and understand these sources. Of the thousands of archives, of the millions of collections held by those archives, there might be half a dozen items of use to you and you're unlikely to find them through random keyword searches. The vast quantity of published academic books and articles can often seem overwhelming and impossible to get to grips with because of their abundance. But the deep stores of information held in archives, buried in datasets and in government records, make the academic literature look like a thin analytical skim on the top of a vast sea of information. It is only through the development of expertise in your subject area, through contact with people who know the sources, and through looking at the sources used by others working in the same area that you will develop knowledge of which archives, which statistical resources and which collections of government documents are likely to be of use to you. It's only with that initial direction that you can effectively search these resources online.

Governments

While governments make many of their publications freely available online, and generally provide very sophisticated search options, it can be difficult to find your way through these vast storehouses of documentation. There are often multiple routes to the same materials. Going to a government site and doing keyword searches is not usually the quickest way to identify relevant government documents.

If you are interested in an issue of current controversy, there are several other routes that are worth trying first. Governments often provide guides to their documentation on current issues and press releases aimed at journalists and an interested public. While these guides are not comprehensive and are often concerned primarily with presenting materials that support the government's case, they can provide a quick introduction to the kinds of official documentation available, suggesting future avenues for searching.

It is useful to supplement this by searching for government documents from the other side of the fence, by using the resources provided by critics of government policy. The workings of government are the direct concern of political activists, non-governmental organizations and elected representatives. All of these have a strong interest in, and knowledge of, government documentation on the issues that concern them.

News stories can also provide a short-cut to government documents. Government policy is the stuff of controversy, debate, dispute and argument, and is therefore the subject of extensive news coverage. News stories can point to the names of key individuals, government reports and key phrases which you can then use as search terms when searching government sources directly.

| Search tip |

Searching for government information by domain

On Google, Yahoo and Bing add **site:gov** to your query to ensure you only search US government sites. Add **site:mil** to restrict it to US military sites. Note that not all government documents are to be found in the official domains. You can use the same syntax to restrict your search to any domain you choose, and you are not limited to top-level domains. Thus **site:gov.uk** will limit your search to UK government sites while **site:fco.gov.uk** will limit it even more narrowly to the site of the UK's Foreign and Commonwealth Office.

In some cases it can be easier and more productive to search government resources via a search engine than to search them directly. A search engine can turn up materials that you'll miss if you search the sites directly. Thus, Google searches the text of pdf documents hosted on government websites while some of these websites don't search their own pdf files – a very significant fact considering that the bulk of published documents placed online are pdf documents.

The British government

In common with many other European governments, the British government has enthusiastically adopted the Internet in the hope and expectation that it will bring government and citizen closer together. The Internet is used to provide detailed information about public services to citizens through *Directgov* (**www.direct.gov.uk**) and to carry out public consultation on government policy proposals. Government publications, records of parliamentary proceedings and government press releases are all available through a variety of overlapping services. Individual government departments provide collections of documents relevant to their responsibilities and there are also several central indexes of government documents.

Key guides include *National Governments* (**www.bl.uk/eresources/socsci/nationalgov.html**), a guide from the British Library covering governments around the world but particularly strong on British government resources. The Keele University guide to *British Government and Politics on the Internet* (**www.keele. ac.uk/depts/por/ukbase.htm**) includes sections on UK government resources.

House of Commons Library Briefing Papers (**www.parliament.uk/business/publications/ research/briefing-papers/**) A collection of research papers on topics of contemporary political controversy put together by staff at the British House of Commons Library to provide summaries of fact and opinion on these issues for British Members of Parliament. They can provide a useful introduction to a topic of current or recent political debate.

UK Parliament (**www.parliament.uk**) The advanced search on the Parliament website (**www.parliament.uk/search/advanced**) allows you to restrict your search to particular types of publication. Select categories such as 'Debates and answers' to get a full list of the various options under this heading. For example, this allows you to limit your search to the text of proceedings in the House of Commons between specific dates from 2001 onwards. You can also search the Parliament site through a search engine such as Google, Bing or Yahoo by limiting your search to **site:publications.parliament.uk**. The search engines don't allow you to restrict the search according to the kinds of material you want to search, however.

Parliamentary Publications and Records (**www.parliament.uk/business/publications/**) This list of publications by the UK Parliament acts as a kind of guide to the materials searchable on the Parliament website, including Hansard and Select Committee Publications.

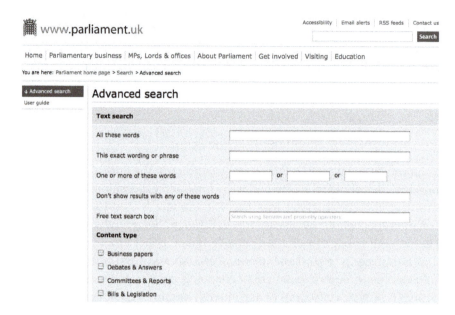

Figure 7.1   UK Parliament website: some options from the advanced search page

Official Documents (**www.official-documents.co.uk**) This includes the full text from the British Government Stationery Office of all command papers, House of Commons papers, and key departmental papers from May 2005 onwards. It also provides a collection of key documents published before that date.

UKOP, the official catalogue of UK official publications since 1980 (**www.ukop.co.uk**) This subscription service includes 450,000 records and is the most comprehensive source of information available on British official publications. It includes the full text of over 30,000 documents.

Search strategy

Searching government sources

Begin a search for government materials by looking for guides produced by the government and by opposition groups to documents on the particular policy you're interested in. These guides will alert you to key collections of documents.

For research on British government policy on Iraq, a quick Google search on **UK government policy Iraq** turns up links to official collections of documents on the topic in the first ten results, including a guide to British government policy produced by the British Foreign and Commonwealth Office. As authoritative and heavily used sources,

---

government sites move to the top of the search results. A key group opposed to US and British policy in Iraq, *IraqWatch*, provides a guide to British government documents on Iraq from a very different perspective. These two guides highlight very different sets of documents but both provide useful starting points.

To find information on a very specific aspect of your topic, you can flexibly combine government sources and keyword search engines. If, for example, you are interested in the way in which the British government drew on its experience in Northern Ireland in dealing with security in Iraq, you could search a range of different sources using the query **"Northern Ireland" Basra**. The city of Basra was the main focus of the British presence in Iraq and provides a very specific search term.

Given that the Foreign and Commonwealth Office (FCO) provides the guide on Iraq policy, you might begin by searching the FCO site. An advanced search, checking the option to 'Include results from all Foreign Office websites' for **Basra "Northern Ireland"** brings back 18 results.

A similar search through Google on **site:fco.gov.uk Basra "Northern Ireland"** brings back around 100 results from the FCO website. The results are not as clearly titled but they include many relevant pages missed by the FCO's own search.

You can also limit your search to the IraqWatch collection of British government documents in Google. **site:www.iraqwatch.org/government "Northern Ireland" Basra** brings back two directly relevant government documents from the IraqWatch site.

A search for **Iraq Basra "Northern Ireland"** on the UK Parliament site that is limited to 'Committees and Reports' from 2001 onwards brings back more than 40 documents. They include evidence given to committees by government ministers talking about the way in which the military used the same techniques in Basra as were used in Northern Ireland.

To search the text of debates in the House of Commons, limit the search to 'Hansard debates'. A search on **Basra "Northern Ireland"** limited to materials from 2001 onwards brings back more than 70 results, including further remarks by ministers and MPs comparing security tactics in Northern Ireland and Iraq.

A search of the Parliament website through Bing does not allow such precise searching: **site:parliament.uk Basra "Northern Ireland"** brings back more than 200 results.

The European Union

All of the European Union member states provide extensive online services of their own, and a list of these national sites is provided on the main EU website along with basic data on each state (**europa.eu/about-eu/countries/**).

European Government Information (**www.lib.berkeley.edu/doemoff/govinfo/foreign/gov_eurogvt.html**) This is a guide from the library at the University of California, Berkeley, cataloguing online resources and documents from several large European states.

The services dealt with below are concerned primarily with the EU itself rather than with the individual member states. EU institutions, and their complex relationship with the national governments of member states, are clearly explained in the services below, and all of them provide guides to the various online storehouses of EU documentation.

Europa (**europa.eu**) The official gateway to EU information sources, including guides to EU institutions, databases of EU documentation, materials organized by subject area, and statistical information.

European Sources Online (**www.europeansources.info**) A commercial online database dealing with the EU and Europe as a whole, it provides introductory guides to European information sources and to EU institutions. Search results are organized by type, identifying them as news items, legislation or reports, for example. It includes official EU information and media reports about the EU.

The US government

The US government has the biggest web presence of any government but it can also lay claim to being one of the most chaotic. There are several different ways of getting access to this information, most of them overlapping but never covering the exact same set of data. It is an entire world of information in its own right and there are professional searchers who devote their careers to finding their way through this documentation.

A useful guide to the world of US federal government documentation (**www. lib.berkeley.edu/doemoff/govinfo/federal/index.html**) is provided by the library at the University of California, Berkeley. It provides brief explanations of the way in which US government institutions work to help you understand the sources you're searching.

State and Local Government on the Net (**www.statelocalgov.net**) This provides links to the thousands of websites of US state, county and city governments.

GPO Access (**www.access.gpo.gov**) This is the online service of the US Government Printing Office, which is legally responsible for printing US government publications. It is the 'official' site for US government publications on the web. However, the GPO is not responsible for the websites of US government agencies or for much of the output of the US Congress. In addition, some US government agencies publish their own materials and these do not come under the care of the GPO. Thus it provides access to a huge range of US government documents but not, by any means, to all of them. GPO Access provides several databases, one of the most important of which is the *Catalog of US Government Publications (CGP)* (**catalog.gpo.gov**) whose Metalib search engine (**metalib.gpo.gov**) searches across numerous US federal government databases simultaneously. Many of the GPO Access databases are also available elsewhere on the web, sometimes in a form that is easier to search and has more comprehensive coverage. In particular, GPO Access overlaps with the official site for the US Congress, THOMAS.

THOMAS (**thomas.loc.gov**) Named after Thomas Jefferson, this service of the Library of Congress provides information related to the US Congress, including information about legislation, transcripts of debates and the reports of congressional committees. The committee reports deal with a vast array of subjects and draw on the testimony of experts. They can be a valuable source of information on issues of political debate in the USA.

Fedworld (**www.fedworld.gov**) This is the official gateway to all US government information online, from official publications through catalogues to government websites. It allows you to search a range of government databases. One of the more useful of these is the NTIS database (National Technical Information Service: **www.ntis.gov**). This is a database of US government reports, or reports funded in part by the US government, including reports produced by university researchers (Basch, 1998: 184). They are available for free or at little cost. Fedworld is good for identifying useful sites that you can then search individually. You can search US government websites via Fedworld, but you can generally do a more precise and complete search of these sites by going directly to them and using their own search options.

USA.Gov (**www.usa.gov**) This is the US government's official web portal, organizing information by organization and topic, and allowing you to jointly search US government websites. It has very useful advanced search facilities. You can limit your search to particular kinds of site and it includes government sites that are not in the .gov or .mil domains.

Lexis Nexis Congressional (**www.lexisnexis.com**) This is a powerful subscription service that indexes publications of the US Congress, providing access to the full text of many of them. Look for a link from your library or institution.

Other governments

There is huge variation in the amount and types of material which governments make available on the web. Many governments have adopted the Internet enthusiastically and put vast amounts of well-organized and valuable information online. This is often aimed primarily at their own citizens as part of a wider aspiration towards the provision of more efficient services to citizens (see Hoff et al., 2000). By contrast, some governments, including many of those with repressive political systems, aim their websites primarily at the outside world, rather than at their own citizens. The agencies which are online tend to be those such as tourist boards, industrial development agencies or government information bureaux, which have a vested interest in contact with foreign investors, tourists and journalists. *The Yahoo Directory* page on 'National Governments' (**dir.yahoo. com/government/countries/**) provides links, organized by country, to official government documents and websites and to websites relating to governments around the world, although it is a little uneven in its coverage.

Archives

Archives used to be quite inaccessible and difficult to use. Because of these difficulties they have been under-utilized as a research resource and many researchers are barely aware that they exist at all. The Internet has facilitated a dramatic opening up of the archives. Collections that could once only be explored and searched by people who went to the archive in person can now be explored online. In addition, universities and governments are scanning and digitizing large volumes of archive materials that could previously only be viewed by visitors to the archive in question.

Although most national archives are dedicated primarily to preserving records of government activity, they also include a wide range of other materials. Archives commonly include the records of organizations and of private individuals, often people who have been prominent in public life. They also host large quantities of rare materials, of which there may only be a few copies still in existence.

Archives consist of materials created by, or received and accumulated by, a person or organization in the course of the conduct of their affairs, and are preserved because of their continuing value. The term has usually been used to refer to non-current records deposited in an archival institution (Ellis, 1993: 2). They exist in a wide variety of formats and can include paper files, photographs, maps, architectural drawings, films, sound recordings and electronic records.

Understanding archives

To search archives effectively you need to understand how they are organized. Archives are generally organized according to the principles of provenance and original order. To preserve their original intellectual integrity, 'records groups' are formed on the principle of preserving together records generated by the same office, department or other bureaucratic cell or person. The principle of original order involves keeping records in the order in which they were accumulated, as they were created, maintained or used, and not rearranging them according to some latterly imposed subject, numerical, chronological or other order (Ellis, 1993: 11). These principles aim to preserve the context of records and a central purpose of archival catalogues is to provide information about these contexts, to trace the history of the various departments and to explain the way in which those organizations and units ordered their records. Archivists provide this contextual information about their holdings in resources known traditionally as 'finding aids'. These finding aids are now available online in many cases. In addition, many archives provide guides to resources on particular topics and often allow the researcher to search archive catalogues by keyword or by subject. Note that you will generally not be searching the full text of documents, but simply the titles and short descriptions of the files. Some archives provide online help, allowing researchers to contact a specialist in a particular area by email.

Guides to online archives

Ready, net go! (**www.tulane.edu/~lmiller/ArchivesResources.html**) A catalogue of the various guides to archives that are available online.

Repositories of primary sources (**www.uidaho.edu/special-collections/Other. Repositories.html**) A simple but useful collection of links to the websites of over 5,000 archives and manuscript repositories around the world, organized geographically.

The National Archives (US) (archives.gov)

As one of the most extensive online archives, this website provides a series of guides on specialized research topics (**archives.gov/publications/findingaids/ guides.html**), including a *Guide to Federal Records in the National Archives of the US.*

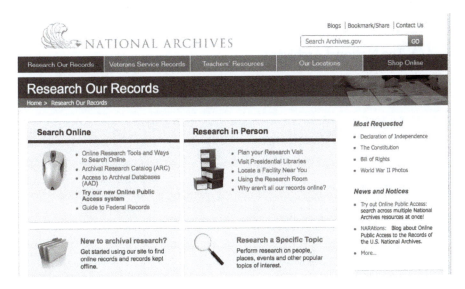

Figure 7.2 The US National Archives' home page for research

ARC (**archives.gov/research/arc/**) This is the main catalogue of the archive's holdings. You can search by keyword, digitized image and location. The advanced search options also allow you to search by organization, person or topic. When you search ARC, you search not only the titles of records but also short descriptions of record groups and sometimes files and individual items. Searches also cover records that have been digitized – a tiny proportion of the total. They include documents and images.

AAD: Access to Archival Databases (**aad.archives.gov/aad**) This is an archive of databases. It makes around 500 of the 200,000 data files held by the US National Archives available online and allows you to search for information about the other data files.

The National Archives (UK) (www.nationalarchives.gov.uk)

The online catalogue of its holdings includes over 8 million document references with descriptions of the documents and descriptions of the classes in which they are categorized. It provides excellent and detailed research guides on a wide range of topics, from sources for the study of Anglo-Jewish history to treaties. The Archives include the *National Digital Archive of Datasets* (NDAD) (**www.nationalarchives.gov.uk/documentsonline/datasets.asp**), which preserves and provides access to computer datasets from UK government departments and agencies. NDAD provides open access to the catalogues of all its holdings, and free access to open datasets. Another service of the British National Archives, *ARCHON* (**www.nationalarchives.gov.uk/archon/**), is a guide to manuscript sources for British history. From here you can access information on all repositories in the UK, and all those repositories throughout the world that have collections of manuscripts which are noted on the British National Register of Archives.

Figure 7.3 UK National Archives: search page

| Search strategy |

Searching an archive

The simplest way to identify relevant archive sources is to look at the key publications in your subject area. Bibliographies and references in these books and articles will give you a good idea of the major archival resources available. These leads can be used, together with the approaches described below, to identify the key sources.

This example illustrates a search for materials in the UK National Archives. Every archive is organized differently but the search nonetheless illustrates some of the general approaches useful in searching archives. In the example, the aim is to identify key collections of records on British policy in Iraq during the 1920s and 1930s, when Britain administered Iraq as a League of Nations 'mandate'.

The first step is to look at the list of the archive's research guides. While none deals specifically with Iraq, a keyword search of the research guides retrieves four guides that mention Iraq. The most useful of these is the guide to sources on the League of Nations. A sub-section in this guide is devoted entirely to the mandates and lists the relevant files on the Iraq mandate, including a range of Colonial Office records: CO 696, CO 730, CO 731, CO 781, CO 782, CO 813. Enter any of these codes in the 'Go to reference' box and you will get a description of the files included under this reference number. The description explains how these particular records fit into the overall administrative structure and briefly describes their contents. It often acts as a pointer to related records that might also be relevant.

You can also search the catalogue by keyword (go to 'Search the archives' and choose 'Search the catalogue'). A general search on **Iraq AND mandate** (limited to the period from 1918 to 1950) returns 20 results. Several of them are from CO 730, which is described as correspondence on Iraq from the 1920s and 1930s. CO 730 includes 178 volumes in total, a massive store of documentation.

Once you have identified the relevant record series, you can limit your searches in the catalogue according to the 'Department or Series code'. Thus, a search on 'Kurds' limited to CO 730 brings back eight files on Kurds in Iraq during the mandate period, all of which are likely to include a wide range of documents.

You can then take a reference number like this and use it to identify books and articles that draw on these archives. This has the dual purpose of getting more information about the contents of these specific files, and pointing users to books that use the archives and are likely to provide pointers to other relevant files on the Iraq mandate.

A search on **"CO 730" Archives Iraq mandate** in Google Scholar returns ten results, almost all of them academic articles or books about the British mandate in the 1920s and 1930s, all of them using archive sources.

In Google Book Search (**books.google.com**), it returns seven recent books, almost all of which are serious historical studies that use archive sources extensively. Between them, these books and articles provide a rich store of information about archive sources on the Iraq mandate from researchers who have already spent time in the archives.

Digital archives

Digital archives aim to make the full text of archival materials available online, rather than simply allowing people to search a catalogue of the materials held. As the major archives begin to scan in parts of their collections, the distinction between traditional archive and digital archive has been eroded. Both *OAIster* (**oaister.worldcat.org**) and Google Scholar (**scholar.google.com**) search digital archives, although you can't limit your search to them. Below are a number of very specialized digital archives that indicate the kinds of resource that are provided on some topics. If there is a digital archive directly relevant to your subject area, it may well be easier to find it through a good subject guide or by word of mouth and personal recommendation than through searching the big search engines.

Chinese Digital Archive 1966–1976 (**anulib.anu.edu.au/subjects/ap/digilib/chi/cr/ china.html**) An archive of photographs, scanned documents and papers focusing on the Chinese Communist Party and the Cultural Revolution. It is maintained by the Australian National University.

The Cornell University Library Witchcraft Collection (**ebooks.library.cornell.edu/w/ witch/digital.html/**) Over many decades Cornell University built up a unique archive of medieval texts on witchcraft. In many cases only a few copies of these books still survive. The full text of more than 100 of these books has been made freely available in this online collection.

American Memory (**memory.loc.gov/ammem/**) A project of the US Library of Congress that focuses on US history. It includes several million digitized images and texts organized in subject-specific collections.

The Online Archive of California (**www.oac.cdlib.org**) The archive draws on the collections of museums, historical societies and archives, and provides over 120,000 images and 50,000 pages of documents, letters and oral histories.

Conflict Archive on the Internet: CAIN (**cain.ulst.ac.uk**) This project of the University of Ulster has archived a huge collection of materials related to violent conflict in Northern Ireland. Through agreement with authors, publishers, organizations and members of the public, it has scanned in pamphlets, posters, leaflets and large private collections of photographs. It has also made the text of a wide range of published journal articles and book chapters, some of them out of print, available free of charge through arrangements with individual authors and publishers.

Statistics

Many researchers will never need to go beyond the statistics presented in published books and academic articles. Even those who do will find most of what they need in the reports by statistical agencies that summarize statistics on various topics. If you do need to explore the statistics in more detail, it's important to know more or less exactly what you're looking for before you start dealing with the raw data.

Statistical bodies provide statistics in a number of different forms. For many researchers it will be more than enough to read the reports analyzing the data, the simplest form in which it is available. You can also get access to statistical tables online, the kinds of table which used to be contained in a government census publication, listing numbers according to age or birthplace or nationality, for example. You can print them out and look at them. They're useful in their own right but they're static. You can't manipulate the data. You can't play around with it and ask for different results.

Increasingly, statistics providers allow you to manipulate and analyze their data on their websites. You can use pull-down menus and query boxes on the websites to crunch the numbers yourself and produce tables customized to your own research needs. This is less flexible than having the data yourself, but it means you have an easy-to-use interface and you don't need to learn how to use a complex piece of statistical software.

Some statistics providers now make the raw statistical data available as data files which you can download to your own computer. You can then open them up on a piece of statistical software such as SPSS and perform very sophisticated analyses of the statistics. This is really only for those with a reasonably advanced knowledge of how to use the statistics. In many cases you can only get access to data files if you are a registered user or if you pay for them, but huge volumes of data are now freely available online nonetheless.

Search strategy

Searching for statistics

Start by searching for academic articles, reports and studies on your topic that use statistical sources. This is one of the simplest ways to identify relevant statistical sources. To identify recent statistics on European attitudes to immigration, for example, search Google Scholar for **attitudes immigration Europe statistics**. Limit the search to articles published after 2005 in the advanced search to exclude earlier articles that use out-of-date statistics.

Among the first few results are a Eurostat report on immigration to the EU (**epp.eurostat.ec.europa.eu**) and items that draw on the Eurobarometer surveys (**ec.europa.eu/**

(Continued)

(Continued)

public_opinion/index_en.htm). This alerts you to the importance of these two key sources on immigration and attitudes to immigration. Other results from the initial Google search refer to the European Social Survey (**www.europeansocialsurvey.org**) and the British Social Attitudes Survey. All of these surveys have generated reports and publications that analyze the data they provide on attitudes to immigration.

You can use the names of any of these surveys, combined with key terms on the topic, to identify further academic work and public debate that refers to these surveys. Thus a Google Scholar search on **"British Social Attitudes" immigration** turns up almost 1,500 sources, many of which draw on the survey for discussions of attitudes to immigration. In Google Book Search, it brings up more than 500 books, including the 27th report of the survey and many other directly relevant books. In Google it turns up tens of thousands of results but virtually all of the first ten are directly relevant academic sources and the results also include many news sources summarizing some of the key conclusions.

A more precise search is possible through ESDS International, part of the UK *Economic and Social Data Service (ESDS)* (**www.esds.ac.uk/international/citations/citations.asp**). It allows you to search for academic publications that cite data from various international surveys, including *Eurobarometer*, the United Nations, the Organization for Economic Cooperation and Development (OECD) and other international datasets. You can limit your search to individual surveys. A search, for example, on *Eurobarometer* and '**immigration**' finds four academic articles on immigration that cite *Eurobarometer* data on the topic.

You can use the text of survey questions to make your search even more specific. One key question in the *Eurobarometer* survey uses the distinctive phrase "the presence of foreigners", which can be used as a specialized search term to identify other articles that refer to this particular question.

Thus a Google search on **"the presence of foreigners" Eurobarometer** generates results that are concerned directly with European attitudes to immigration. Among these results are several reports from Europa, the central European site that hosts *Eurobarometer*.

Guides to statistical sources

Offstats (**www.offstats.auckland.ac.nz**) This links to official statistical resources worldwide, organized geographically and by topic. It is a service of the University of Auckland library.

The US Bureau of Labour Statistics (**www.bls.gov/bls/other.htm**) This provides an extensive list of the websites of government statistical agencies around the world.

The *Guardian* (**www.guardian.co.uk/world-government-data**) The site for this UK newspaper allows you to do a joint search of a wide variety of government data sites from their 'World Government data' page.

Among the most sophisticated and elaborate national data sites available in English (wholly or partially) are those of the USA (**data.gov**), Australia (**data.australia.gov.au**), New Zealand (**data.govt.nz**), the UK (**data.gov.uk**), Canada (**www.statcan.gc.ca**), Germany (**www.destatis.de**) and Finland (**www.stat.fi/index_en.html**). Note that in federal jurisdictions such as Germany and the USA many of the most important datasets are compiled and managed by the statistical agencies of the component states.

UK statistics

National Statistics (**www.statistics.gov.uk**) is the Official UK statistics website, organizing material by subject areas, such as migration, education and economy. The site provides information about newly released datasets.

European Union statistics

The European Union's statistical role is focused on coordinating and harmonizing statistical work by the official statistics bodies in its member states. These national statistics offices are listed in the guides mentioned above. *Eurostat* (**epp.eurostat.ec.europa.eu**), the European Union's Statistical Information Service, takes the lead role in this and produces statistical reports based on data from the various member states. The European Union does gather its own data in some areas. For example, *Eurobarometer* (**ec.europa.eu/public_opinion/index_en.htm**), the Public Opinion Analysis sector of the European Commission, carries out regular surveys of public opinion across the EU, dealing with contemporary political issues. It provides reports summarizing the results.

US statistics

USA.Gov provides a 'Data and Statistics' section that provides a useful guide to US government data and statistical resources (**www.usa.gov/Topics/Reference_Shelf/Data.shtml**). One of the central sources of statistical data on the USA is the *US Census Bureau* (**www.census.gov**) (see Figure 7.4). *FedStats* (**www.fedstats.gov**) provides a guide to the statistical data produced by over 100 US federal government agencies, organized by subject and geographically. It provides links to statistical publications and reports, and you can search individual agencies or search them jointly.

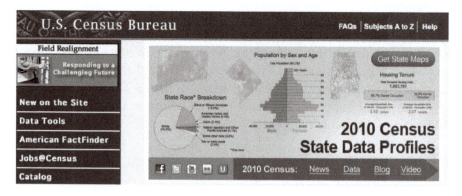

Figure 7.4 US Census Bureau home page

International statistics

The UN Statistics Division (**unstats.un.org/unsd**) This provides a range of statistical databases drawing together data from national statistical agencies around the world on topics such as housing, population and gender. They also provide a number of subscription databases.

OECD iLibrary (**www.oecd-ilibrary.org**), the Organization for Economic Cooperation and Development's Online Library, includes a large number of international statistical databases on employment, health, education, international migration and trade.

Data archives

Data archives hold and preserve datasets gathered by a wide variety of organizations and research projects. In many cases they allow users to download the full datasets to analyze them on their own computers. Data files may exist in a definitive version and be generated by a project or business function with a finite timespan, or a data file may be dynamic, constantly evolving, generated by a project or business function with no finite timescale (Feeney, 1999: 10).

The Economic and Social Data Service (ESDS) (**www.esds.ac.uk**) This is a UK academic data service that provides access to a vast collection of both qualitative and quantitative data across the social sciences. It includes data from large-scale UK government surveys and a range of European and international surveys.

ICPSR: The Inter-university Consortium for Political and Social Research (**www.icpsr.umich. edu**) ICPSR provides access to the world's largest archive of computerized social science data. Access to the datasets is restricted to those affiliated to member colleges and universities. Everybody can get access to abstracts and other documentation related to many of the datasets. You can search for datasets by subject, title and keyword.

CESSDA: Council for European Social Science Data Archives (**www.cessda.org**) Cessda allows you to simultaneously search the catalogues of data archives in several countries, mostly in Europe, but also including the ICPSR in the USA, providing access to more than 25,000 data collections. It also provides links to these catalogues.

The UK Data Archive (**www.data-archive.ac.uk**) An extensive collection of more than 5,000 datasets and related documentation in the social sciences and humanities. The collection consists mainly of datasets that were gathered in the course of publicly funded research projects in the UK. Many of these are surveys carried out by government agencies or public bodies. You can search by subject and keyword. You can view frequencies from popular surveys and most datasets are freely available to anyone. Alongside the large statistical datasets, it includes interview and focus group transcripts and historical data. It provides access for academic researchers in the UK to some of the ICPSR datasets and to European-based data archives. It also provides advice and tutorials online.

Slightly different from the services mentioned above, *The Survey Question Bank* (**surveynet.ac.uk/sqb**) is a UK academic service that provides a store of searchable questionnaires and allows you to explore the questions used in previous surveys as well as learning about the history of individual surveys, their aims and their methods. It also provides a collection of factsheets on survey methods.

Exercises

Exercise 1: Government information

Identify a government likely to have produced materials relevant to your research. Search for guides to government documents on your research topic produced by this government and by a group opposed to this government's policy in that area.

1 Identify the government department or unit most directly concerned with your topic.
2 Search its website to identify documents or collections of documents relevant to your research.
3 Search the same website using the same search terms via two of the following services:

   o Google
   o Yahoo
   o Bing

4 Briefly describe the differences between the first five results of these different searches.

5 Search the proceedings of the relevant legislature/parliament/assembly using very specific keywords related to your topic.
6 Search the reports of legislative/parliamentary committees using the same keywords.
7 Briefly describe the results. How useful were these searches?
8 Briefly describe the search process as a whole, the most productive part of the search, the difficulties you encountered, and any advice you would give to someone else embarking on a similar search.

Exercise 2: Searching archives

Find an academic article or book relevant to your research that uses archive sources. Use that article or book to identify an archive that is likely to hold materials relevant to your research, and to identify records that might be relevant.

1 Search for a research guide at that archive that deals with your subject area and use it to identify key records.
2 Identify other relevant records by searching the archive using broad search terms related to your topic.
3 Identify further relevant records by searching the archive using very specific terms related to your topic.
4 Describe the overlap and the differences between the results produced by these four different search methods.
5 Go to the descriptions of several of the most promising-looking records you have identified through these searches. Pick out two or three record series or files that are most likely to be of use to you.
6 Use the reference codes for these files, the term 'archives', and a key term associated with your topic area to search in the following sources for publications that use these archives. If the code for an individual file is too specific to retrieve results, use the code for the record series that file belongs to, in order to make the search broader.

   o Google Scholar
   o Google Books

Describe the results. How useful are they?
7 Carry out the same search in two of the search engines below:

   o Bing
   o Yahoo
   o Google

Describe and compare the results from the two services. How useful are they?
8 Briefly describe the search process as a whole, the most productive part of the search, the difficulties you encountered, and any advice you would give to someone else embarking on a similar search.

Exercise 3: Statistics

Search for academic articles and books relevant to your research that use statistical data. Use these publications to identify a statistical source relevant to your research.

1 Use the names of this source, combined with one or two key terms on your topic, to identify further academic work and reports that refer to this source. Search in the following services:

 o Google Scholar
 o Google Books

2 Find the web pages for the statistical source and identify the relevant reports on your topic (search Google, Yahoo or Bing for the name of the survey or agency and, if necessary, the topic).

3 Using the name of the source and a distinctive phrase from one of the survey questions that relates directly to your topic, search for sources that make direct reference to this question. Search in the following services:

 o Google Scholar
 o Google Books

Briefly describe the results. How useful are they?

4 Do the same search in at least two of these services:

 o Google
 o Yahoo
 o Bing

Describe and compare the results from the two services. How useful are they?

5 Briefly describe the search process as a whole, the most productive part of the search, the difficulties you encountered, and any advice you would give to someone else embarking on a similar search.

EIGHT

Evaluation and citation

Introduction

Lies and propaganda have always been with us. They don't originate with the Internet and they're not confined to the Internet. However, the Internet does ensure that academic researchers and students are less insulated from highly problematic sources than they used to be (see Mintz, 2002). A central, if largely invisible, function of publishers and libraries is to exclude, screening out a huge range of materials in the process of selecting resources for publication or purchase. This ongoing work of exclusion shielded researchers and students from a huge proportion of the information circulating in the world. Now that we have access to a much wider range of sources, we have to develop new skills to evaluate them. It is necessary to become much more sensitive to the wide range of signals that provide an indication of the character and reliability of an online source. The new information environment necessitates a much more actively critical approach to the sources we use.

In judging information sources, we draw unconsciously on a wide range of visual and contextual cues. We are more inclined to rely on a footnoted book from a university press located in a university library than on a scribbled note written on the back of a stained beer-mat in a bar. The academic book might be a discredited work, subsequently shown to be riddled with errors. The beer-mat note might have been written by one of the foremost experts in the field, but their appearance and location will play a powerful role in determining our judgement of them.

The visual and contextual clues that help us to make a judgement on the reliability of a source are not completely absent online but they are far less obvious.

The online equivalents of the beer-mat note and the academic book are much closer in appearance than their offline counterparts. Evaluating online sources requires developing your awareness of a range of much subtler indications of a source's reliability. This is not to suggest that all academic sources are reliable and unbiased, or to imply that non-academic sources as a whole are not. Like their offline counterparts, the online equivalent of the beer-mat may well be a more useful and relevant source to you than the online equivalent of the academic book.

Because it can be so much more difficult to evaluate the reliability of online sources and because they are so much less controlled than the resources available in a library, many in academia express extreme scepticism of the value of any online source. There is a tendency to seek to resolve the issues around evaluation and quality by excluding Internet sources. Much of this scepticism is well founded, but the response to these challenges is not to turn away from online sources. Instead, it is important to develop critical information literacy, a new set of skills to help us to develop a better understanding of the materials we are looking at, to allow us to evaluate authority and credibility and to understand the context in which materials have been produced.

Classification

A useful starting point for evaluating online sources is to begin with a rough classification of the materials you are dealing with. Classifying involves putting a document in a necessarily crude category in order to be able to assess it according to the standards appropriate to that category. When you've decided a document is a news document, you won't be disappointed that it's not footnoted. You won't expect an advocacy document to be neutral. Conversely, when an academic document clearly falls short of the standards of proof that you expect of such materials, you have a right to be particularly sceptical of its conclusions. The categories given here are necessarily crude and you will find that a lot of web pages are difficult to fit into one category or another. The guidelines below are not intended as a set of rigid instructions to be followed mechanically, but as a series of questions that can usefully be asked about any online materials. Doing this is valuable in itself, allowing you to develop a better understanding of the nature of the source.

Advocacy

Advocacy groups, such as political parties, non-governmental organizations or pressure groups, advocate a particular cause or viewpoint. They weigh up competing arguments as they develop these positions, but that process of weighing up is not their prime concern. The advancement of a particular point of view is their core purpose.

Some advocacy groups systematically and deliberately distort and exaggerate facts in pursuit of their aims. On the other hand, many advocacy groups produce work of extremely high quality. The work of groups such as the *Minority Rights Group* (**www.minorityrights.org**) and *Amnesty International* (**www.amnesty.org**) draws on academic standards while also seeking to have a direct political impact. They are valuable academic resources and we need to be careful not to approach all advocacy documents with unduly high levels of scepticism.

Generally, you will recognize an advocacy document because it will be clearly marked with the name of the group that produced it. If not, the name of the group should be there on the site home page. Although many advocacy groups use the **.org** domain, not all such groups do, so the URL does not provide a reliable guide, although many try to avoid the **.com** domain. Be aware that some advocacy groups try to give their arguments more credibility by making themselves sound like academic organizations with titles like the 'Centre for research on ...' or the 'Institute for the study of ...'.

It can be difficult to distinguish an advocacy document from a personal page since so many individuals put up pages advocating particular views. An individual may well set up an organization of which he or she is the founder, president and sole member. In the sense in which I use the term, such a one-person show should not be considered an advocacy group and their output on the web should be treated as personal pages rather than advocacy documents. They should be treated with the especially high levels of caution appropriate for such pages.

Advocacy documents are problematic mainly because they often only give one side of a story. There is one simple and obvious way to correct this imbalance – get the other side of the story. If an advocacy group is on the web, it's likely their opponents are also online.

Academia

Academic documents undergo some sort of quality control, whether it is the examination process a thesis or dissertation goes through, the peer review which journal articles are subject to, or the editorial process academic books go through. Academic documents are accorded a certain degree of authority because of the experience of authors, reflected in their academic qualifications and their other publications. This isn't to say that all academic work is perfect; merely that it has gone through a set of procedures that provide at least some sort of quality control.

Academia attracts a certain amount of respect, as a source of unbiased research. As a result, certain advocacy groups, businesses and news sources try to make their documents look like academic documents. Several countries have domains which are reserved for academic institutions, **edu** in the USA, **ac.uk** in Britain, **ac.jp** in Japan, **edu.au** in Australia, for example. In other countries, the universities are easily recognized by their web addresses. In Germany, **www.uni-oldenburg.de** is Oldenburg University, **www.uni-heidelberg.de** is Heidelberg University, and so on.

Not all documents on university servers are academic documents. The mountains of materials that universities provide about themselves are best classified as 'official' documents (see below). Many universities also allow students to create websites on the university's web server. These are personal pages (see below), and in some cases advocacy documents, and should be treated as such.

There are now large numbers of academic draft papers and works in progress on the web. Although these are clearly academic documents, you cannot treat them like published articles. In many cases authors stipulate that you should not quote from or cite these articles without direct permission from the author. You can read them and print them, but you can only cite them after you go to the trouble of contacting the author, assuming your own supervisor is happy for you to use materials which haven't taken final form.

Official documents

Official documents are those produced by public institutions, and by government and international agencies. They include documents from the smallest local council or fire department up to national bodies such as government departments and agencies. They include documents from international organizations, from the UN and OPEC to NATO and the OSCE.

Many governments have their own domain (**gov** in the USA, **gov.uk** in Britain, **gov.jp** in Japan) or their government affiliation is often clear from their URL. In Germany and in Denmark, for example, government ministries have web addresses that include abbreviations of the ministries' titles. The German Environment Ministry, the BMU, is **www.bmu.de**, while the URL for the Irish government is **www.irlgov.ie**. Many US states have their own domains. Thus **ca.gov** is the domain for the California state government. Some US states have domains that do not come under the overall **gov** domain, such as New York State, whose domain is **state.ny.us**. Government domains in most cases only cover central government. Local and regional bodies often make their own arrangements and it is not as straightforward to identify them by their URLs. Political considerations do of course influence official documents, and in certain cases they shade over into clear advocacy of particular positions.

The boundary between official and news sources can be unclear. Many countries have official news agencies connected to government, such as Xinhua in China. Despite being government agencies, their prime function is to provide news. Apart from this, many governments issue press releases and print publications to promote the government currently in power. These are not news services but they sometimes look like they are, particularly on the web where it's easy to put together a collection of government statements and call them a news bulletin or news update.

News

Traditional news sources such as wire services, newspapers, TV and radio news programmes and magazines are being joined by new media sources such as news blogs and alternative online news sources, such as Indymedia (**www.indymedia.org**). The line between government and advocacy groups and news sources can be quite unclear at times. News sources do tend to be informed by a particular political viewpoint. This is reflected in the way they cover news stories, in the stories they choose to cover, in the aspects of a story they emphasize and in the editorial positions they take. In many cases news sources have more direct political affiliations. If you are using an unfamiliar news source, you need to be aware that many news sources across the world are directly linked to political parties or governments, and their approach to the news can be even more partisan than you would usually expect from a news source. Many new media sources are much more openly partisan in their coverage than traditional media.

Most online newspapers still follow the basic layout of the print version – a front page with short summaries of stories that appear inside – so that you recognize them as news sources immediately from their familiar layout. Likewise, the websites of TV news services are clearly identified. The wire services provide news stories to huge numbers of other web services but they always clearly stamp their name on the individual news stories. These are news documents no matter what kind of site they appear on.

As with academia, the news media has a reasonably high level of credibility. Some advocacy groups imitate the style, layout and terminology of news documents in an attempt to increase their credibility.

News sources, like academia, aspire to the pursuit of truth and the ideal of objectivity. Unlike academia, news sources set lower formal standards of proof and referencing of sources. They are not footnoted. They can and do give the opinions of individuals as though they represent the opinions of an entire group. Standards vary from one news organization to another, and those papers that attempt to be papers of record, recording all significant events with the intention of acting as a source for researchers in the future, are invaluable as research sources. Many news sources have only the barest consideration for the ideals of objectivity and put considerably more weight on another core purpose of news-gathering: the selling of news as a product.

Personal pages

The recent expansion of services such as Myspace and Bebo has made it a simple matter for anyone with Internet access to set up their own web page and blog. Millions of children, teenagers and adults have web pages that are primarily concerned with their private lives. Many people use their web pages to express their personal opinions on matters of public debate, but few of them expect that others will rely on these private pages as authoritative sources of information. The informal tone and presentation mark these contributions to public debate as essentially private expressions of opinion.

There are a number of crude measures for assessing the value and reliability of a personal page. As the product of a single individual, its reliability will depend on this individual alone. You can look for indicators of how much trust to place in them. Consider what their qualifications to write on the subject are. These qualifications can range from academic degrees to direct personal experience to previous publications on the topic. Finally, evaluate them for accuracy and objectivity, as outlined below.

Business/marketing pages

These are pages set up by commercial companies with the core purpose of selling a product and promoting the company. While they may provide useful information about the company, this information is there to promote the company and its products. When using such pages you have to be constantly aware of this fact and of the very important consequences it has for the reliability of the information provided. Be aware that businesses do sometimes try to present their materials as 'news' or 'research' to give it more credibility.

The **.com** domain was created for businesses and is used by businesses worldwide. In addition, many countries outside the USA have their own commercial domains, such as **.co.uk** in the UK. Just because a site has a **.com** address doesn't automatically make it a business/marketing site, however. Many news organizations, advocacy groups and private individuals use the **.com** domain.

Evaluation

One of the main purposes of evaluating online materials is to judge how trustworthy or reliable a source they are. A second purpose is to identify the sort of information which is immediately obvious in print publications – information about the publisher and author. This information is essential if you are to cite online materials accurately. What follows is a series of checklists to help you assess authority, accuracy, objectivity, currency and quality. It draws heavily on the categories used by Alexander and Tate (1999), elaborating on and reorganizing the categories a little. Don't apply these evaluation criteria too rigidly. Sometimes the most reliable and authoritative of web pages do not include the basic information mentioned in these checklists. Governments, for example, often neglect to stamp their authority clearly on many documents. They often don't bother with footnoting, copyright statements or contact details. It illustrates the fact that those with most authority often feel the least need to proclaim it.

Authority

The author, the organization or institution he or she is associated with and the publisher of the work are the main sources of authority for print publications, in varying degree. Details for each of these are usually provided in print publications.

On a web page, author, organization and publisher can easily be combined in the one person and they can often be quite difficult to identify. There are several questions one can ask.

a) Is it clear who is responsible for the document?

Responsibility may lie with an individual author, an organization or the website owners or publishers. If you can't find this information on the document you're looking at, check if it's available on the front page for that site. The author of a website or blog may simply have copied and pasted information from somewhere else. He or she may well have altered it and given incorrect information about it. In this case you need to track down the original.

b) Is there any information about the person or organization responsible for the page?

Is there any information that would help you to make a judgement about how reliable the author is? In print publications the very fact that a book has been published by a well-established publisher with a good reputation, or has been written by someone with a qualification in the subject they're writing on, lends it a certain credibility. If you're unsure of the quality of the page, you might look to see if any information has been provided about the author or the organization.

3. Is there a copyright statement?

In the absence of a clear statement of who the author is, a copyright statement provides an alternative indication of who is responsible for the document. Don't be too upset if you don't find a copyright statement. Many people don't bother because materials are automatically copyrighted to their author regardless of whether they include a copyright statement or not.

4. Does it have a print counterpart that reinforces its authority?

Print documents in general are regarded as more reliable than web documents. If a web document also has a print version, that is, if it has appeared in a print publication such as a book, journal or newspaper, it reinforces its authority.

Accuracy

There are several questions users can ask to assure themselves of the accuracy of sources.

1. Are sources clearly listed so they can be verified?

This is a fundamental requirement of academic literature, in the form of foot-notes and bibliographies. Although you can't expect non-academic documents to follow academic footnoting conventions, you can usefully pose this question of all documents. You can use it as a measure of the quality and reliability of advocacy documents in particular.

2. Is there an editorial input?

An editor provides an extra layer of quality control which should lead to increased accuracy. Most print publications have been through an editorial process.

3. Is spelling and grammar correct?

You should be careful not to place too much weight on spelling and grammar. Minor errors creep into virtually every publication. However, poor spelling and grammar can indicate a certain carelessness that might affect the document in other ways. If an author has got his or her spelling wrong, then maybe they have got some of the facts wrong too.

Objectivity

It is unrealistic to expect anyone writing on the human and the social world in which all of us are immersed to be detached and objective about their subject. In recent years many in academia have argued against the ideals of detached objectivity on the grounds that it often serves to mask prejudice and bias in the research community. The aspiration to objectivity, however impossible it may be to achieve, is a traditional value of academic research. In practical terms it means that you should not allow your personal preferences to interfere with your research, that you should not distort evidence, that you should not make wild claims based on weak evidence and not deliberately omit evidence. You are entitled to expect academic documents to make more of an attempt at objectivity than, for example, advocacy documents. But just because a document doesn't attempt to be objective doesn't render it worthless. The questions below can usefully be applied to a wide range of documents.

1. Are biases and affiliations clearly stated?

You can expect that an advocacy document will advocate a particular position. The real problem arises when they do not make this clear.

2. Is advertising clearly differentiated from information?

Advertisers often try to present ads in the form of newspaper articles or research findings to give them more credibility. This is deliberately misleading and seriously undermines the credibility of a document.

Currency

Currency means checking the date when the document was produced or last updated to see how up to date it is. If you want to know about the current state of the Nicaraguan economy, for example, it's very important that the documents you're relying on should be as up to date as possible.

In many cases it's not important to the researcher that a document is current. However, it's still important to identify the date when a document was produced. It identifies the historical context for the document. Thus, it's important to know whether a document dealing with the Second World War was produced in the midst of the war, shortly after it or many years later. The period in which it was produced will have a powerful influence on the document, and knowing the date will help you to understand the document. Here are some questions to be aware of.

1. If the document has a print counterpart, is there a date of publication for that?

If there is a print counterpart, and the web version is an unaltered copy of the print version, then the date of the print publication is the only significant date. It's generally irrelevant when it was put on the web or when you viewed it.

2. Are there dates for when the document was first produced or first put on the web?

For a web document with no print counterpart, the dates when it was first produced or first put on the web are two different ways of determining when it was first 'published'.

3. Are there dates for when the document was last updated or revised?

For those documents that are regularly updated it's important to indicate which version you are referring to. The date when it was last updated also indicates how current and up to date the document is. Note that most web authors don't bother to 'constantly update' the documents they put on the web.

Evaluating personal messages and forwarded documents

It can be tricky to assess the reliability of personal messages and forwarded documents as research sources. Personal messages stand on their own merits. You place as much reliability on them as you would on the person who sent them. The same applies to messages sent or posted by organizations and institutions. You trust these messages as much as you trust the organization that sent them.

Things become more difficult when you're dealing with forwarded messages or messages posted to a blog or social network. People often post or forward news stories or other items they've gleaned from the web. In some cases people edit or alter the stories, for legitimate reasons, highlighting the section they want to bring to your attention. In many cases, though, people edit to make news reports appear more favourable to their argument or political position. Be wary of quoting from an item that has been forwarded to you in the body of an email message or as part of a post. You need to check the original and cite the original wherever possible.

The sunscreen speech and the dangers of relying on email messages

In July or August 1997 someone sent an email message that included the text of a short speech which began with the words: 'Wear sunscreen. If I could offer you only one tip for the future, sunscreen would be it.' They described it as a speech that the science-fiction author Kurt Vonnegut had given at a commencement ceremony at the Massachusetts Institute of Technology (MIT) in Boston. It was a clever speech and a lot of people forwarded it on to friends via email. People put copies of it on websites, attributing authorship to Vonnegut. It came to the attention of filmmaker Baz Luhrman (*Romeo and Juliet*, *Strictly Ballroom*, *Moulin Rouge*), who decided to record a song using the text of the speech. When he started searching the Internet for contact details for Vonnegut, so that he could buy the rights to the words, he came across web pages that discussed the speech. It turned out that Kurt Vonnegut had never made such a speech, had never in fact spoken at an MIT commencement ceremony. Columnist Mary Schmich had written the original piece as a column in the *Chicago Tribune* in June 1997. Why the person who first included it in an email message described it as a speech by Vonnegut is a mystery, but as a result thousands of people believed Vonnegut had said it. The moral of the story? Be careful of anything that has been forwarded to you by email. Do your best to find the original source of the information.
  Source: Ahrens (1999)

Citation

The central purposes of citation are to acknowledge your sources, to provide information about the sources that help us to understand the context in which they were produced (such as date, publisher and author), and to make it possible for the reader to track down and consult the original sources. When you're citing online sources you need to bear in mind these core purposes. A URL on its own does not acknowledge the author, does not provide much information about the source and is often not sufficient to guide a reader back to the original source. Authors change their web pages. They move them to new URLs. They delete them.

The spread of reference management software in the past five years has changed citation practices beyond recognition. We are rarely required now to carefully figure out how to reference particular items because we can simply choose a citation style in EndNote or Mendeley or Refworks and let the software figure it out. However, all of these software packages still have difficulties with references to various kinds of online resources and you may frequently find yourself having to tweak and edit certain references.

No matter how carefully you cite Internet sources, you can never guarantee that your reader will be able to access those sources. You can insure yourself against the disappearance of your sources by systematically saving copies of all of the online sources you plan to cite. One of the best ways to do this is through WebCite (**www.webcitation.org**), a free archiving service specifically catering to academic researchers. It is endorsed by hundreds of academic journals and is a member of the International Internet Preservation Consortium. Just paste the URL of the page you want to archive into the WebCite archive form (**www.webcitation.org/archive.php**). WebCite then provides you with a unique URL for the archived copy. You can add this URL to the citation for the page ('archived at…'), thus ensuring that readers can access the page exactly as it was on the day you looked at it. WebCite can archive a wide range of online materials; everything from blogs to Twitter feeds. If you find yourself using it regularly, bookmark the "WebCite this" bookmarklet. You can then archive documents, along with citation details, with a single click. The research management tool, Mendeley (**www.mendeley.com**) also allows you to archive web pages and import citation details with a single click by adding the 'Mendeley Web Importer' to your bookmarks toolbar. Similar easy-to-use facilities are provided by Zotero (**www.zotero.com**) and Evernote (**www.evernote.com**).

In addition, all of the major web browsers allow you to save web pages. If you want to make sure you have archived all of the complex elements of a site, Adobe Acrobat and Internet Explorer have sophisticated web page archiving capacities and there are also many specialized web archiving software packages, including DeepVacuum, WebHTTrack and WebReaper. For the great majority of researchers, however, WebCite or the facilities to save web documents that are built into research management software such as Mendeley or Zotero are more than adequate. If a source disappears or changes and you haven't saved it, you can always try searching the Internet Archive (**www.archive.org**) for a copy. This advice does not apply to online documents that have print counterparts, such as books, articles or reports. It is not as important to save them. They are not likely to disappear or be altered in the same way that web pages are.

If an item that you find online has a print counterpart, cite the print version according to normal citation guidelines. This applies in particular to books, academic journals, and newspaper and magazine articles. The fact that you access these sources online is irrelevant. Some of the most authoritative citation guidelines initially recommended that you cite the database in which you found an academic article or book, the full URL for that database and the date you accessed it. This is excessive and makes citations unnecessarily long. It's like asking you to identify the library shelf you found a book on and to describe the weather at the time. It is not necessary to guide the reader to the original source and it does not add to our understanding of the item. Thankfully, some of those in charge of citation guidelines seem to have realized this and have altered the guidelines accordingly in recent years. Some citation guidelines, such as those of the American Psychological Association (APA) and the *Chicago Manual of Style*, recommend that you include the digital object identifier (DOI) in all citations of online articles. The DOI is a unique code (such as 10.1086/599249) that provides a persistent link to an item's location on the Internet so that you can connect to it even if its online location is changed. Those responsible for some other citation systems omit the DOI and clearly regard this as excessive and unnecessary. To this writer it seems analogous to including the library classification number or ISBN with a reference to a printed book. Yes, it may help the reader to locate the item, but it seems excessive to insist that such information be included with every reference. Unfortunately, if your institution, department or supervisor insists that you follow a style that demands these elements, you will have no choice but to include this redundant information. If you are citing an article from a journal with no print counterpart, you should provide the URL, indicating that this is a purely online source.

If you can't properly cite the materials you use, if you can't mark out a path that will allow the reader to find the original sources you're referring to, they will be entitled to be sceptical of those sources. The very fact that you will be able to assess and cite web documents according to rigorous academic standards is the most powerful argument you can have against the scepticism of those who are suspicious of any Internet-based source.

Emerging citation standards

In recent years some of the main authorities responsible for setting standards for the citation of print documents have laid down guidelines for Internet citation. The *Chicago Manual of Style* provides an excellent 'Quick Guide' to their citation system that includes examples of citations for online materials, including blog posts, websites, online journal articles and email messages (**www.chicagomanualofstyle.org/tools_citationguide.html**).

The publication manual of the *American Psychological Association (APA)* (**www.apastyle.org/manual/index.aspx**) provides well-developed guidelines on 'electronic references'. The APA also provides a few online tutorials and an FAQ that provides guidelines on dealing with some of the trickier aspects of citing online materials, including how to cite Facebook, Twitter and personal email messages (**www.apastyle.org/learn/faqs/index.aspx**).

The Modern Languages Association Handbook (**www.mlahandbook.org**) provides detailed guidelines on citing online sources. The MLA doesn't appear to make any of this information freely available online but a web search on **MLA**

internet citation guidelines will bring back examples and advice from numerous university libraries. To find a wide variety of advice sheets on citation from university libraries, search any search engine for the style you want to use and words such as **citation, style, guide,** or **guidelines**: try **Chicago Manual of Style Citation Guide**, for example.

The examples of citation given below use the author–date referencing system, also known as the Harvard system. It is very widely used in the social and physical sciences. It is used here to illustrate the main elements needed in the citation of online sources rather than to lay down a single standard. These guidelines provide useful advice no matter what citation style you use. Make sure that the citation style you use conforms to the guidelines laid down by your institution, department or supervisor.

Citation elements

To cite a web page or a blog post you need to use most of the elements of a book citation, adapted to suit the Internet. You also need to identify the wider context

Table 8.1 Citation elements for online and offline sources

Citation elements	Book	Article	Web page	Blog entry	Public email/ post
Author	X	X	X	X	X
Year	X	X	X	X	X
Title	X	X (of the article)	X (of the page)	X (of the entry)	X (the subject header or discussion title)
Journal		X			
Site			X (the website it belongs to)	X (the name of the blog)	X (the group or email list)
Volume		X			
Issue		X			
Pages		X			
Place	X				
Publisher	X				
URL			X	X	X (for a group)
Date			X (date viewed/ accessed. Only if essential: see below)	X (the date the entry was posted)	X (the date the email was sent or the post was posted)

in which the online item is located, as you have to do with a print journal article. In the case of an academic article, that context is the journal it appeared in. On the web that wider context is the website a document belongs to, or the blog an entry was made in. In the case of email messages and posts to discussion groups, that wider context is the email list a message belongs to (where applicable) or the group a message was posted to. The other additional element in an Internet citation is the URL. It can be particularly difficult to deal with dates in citing online materials and this issue is dealt with in more detail below. Some citation systems recommend that you include the 'format' of a cited item, labelling it [blog] or [web] or [online] for example, but the boundary between such formats can sometimes be unclear and the fact that it is an online source is already evident from the URL. 'Format' seems an unnecessary element except for the citation of non-print items such as photographs or films and it is not included here in citations of web pages and blogs.

Table 8.1 above compares the different elements used in citing print sources, such as books and articles, and those used in citing online sources.

Author

Authors of blog posts, email messages and posts to discussion groups or social networks are clearly identified, even if that identity is often a nickname or pseudonym. The authors of web pages can be more difficult to identify. If the author of a web page is not clearly identified on the document, check the home page of the site to see if the author is identified there. If the document is produced by an organization, whether that be a government, an advocacy group or a business firm, it may well be that the organization itself is the author. You can assume this if no author is specified. In the case of news items, journalists are often not given a by-line, that is, their name does not appear with the article. In that case, you do not need to give an author name. The news agency or publication is effectively the author and they will appear in the citation in any case.

Title

All web documents have a 'title' field the author can fill in. This is what appears in the bar at the very top of your browser. Many authors don't fill it in and many who do put a different title here from the one visible on the page itself. If the two are different, you should probably use the title which is visible on the page. If it looks like the title, it probably is the title.

Site

When you cite a published journal article, you always include the name of the journal in which it was published. It is equally important in web citation that you cite the website a document belongs to, or the blog a message was posted to. It explains the wider context in which the item is located. Refer back to Chapter 4 for a detailed explanation of what constitutes a site if you have difficulty in identifying it.

URL

There are a few complications around citing URLs. Many services create pages 'on-the-fly', that is, the page is created for you in response to your request. For example, a news service with a huge archive of news stories may offer you the option of clicking on stories on crime. The page it retrieves is not a pre-existing web page which would have its own URL. Rather, it is the result of a search query. The URL will reflect this, being very long, full of numbers and making no sense. In this case, it is often impractical and of little use to cite the URL and it's more important to note details of author, title and site.

Frames can cause major problems for web citation by obscuring the URLs of the pages you are looking at. If you keep seeing the same URL in the bar at the top of the browser as you move to different pages, then this is the URL of the frame itself, not the pages you're looking at. To see the URL, print out the document (ensuring that the print preferences are set to include the URL) or use 'back' to return to the previous page and scan over the link to see the URL. To bookmark an individual page within a framed site so you can check the URL of the bookmark, right-click on the page itself and choose 'add bookmark'.

Given that the vast majority of URLs begin with **http://**, you can omit that part of the URL in your citations. None of the major search engines require you to enter **http://** when you enter the URL and it is therefore unnecessary in directing people back to the source.

Date

For many online documents only one date is needed for a citation, the date when the document was first written or the closest equivalent, such as the date it was first put on the web. A huge proportion of documents are neither changed nor updated after they go on to a website and the date when you viewed these pages is irrelevant. If a document is subject to change, you need to include the date when it was last updated, if it is provided on the page. This indicates the version of the document that you saw. You are not guaranteeing that the document will look the same after the next update.

The third type of date is only relevant to undated documents or to documents that change but do not provide a 'last updated' date, through neglect or carelessness. In this case, and in this case only, you should put down the date on which you viewed it. In the examples below, the term 'accessed' is used. The APA citation guidelines suggest the word 'retrieved'. Whichever word you choose, be sure to use it consistently. This date indicates that you are citing the document as it appeared on the day you viewed it. You are not guaranteeing that it will look the same after that date. When a document is undated, use 'n.d.' (no date) for the year of publication, as in the first example below.

The examples below illustrate four different forms that the citation of a web page might take, depending on the information it provides about dates and on whether it is subject to updating. It's a document called 'Small victories in the kitchen' by an imaginary author, Anna Lee, one of several documents by the author on a site called *Rat Wars*.

No information about dates is provided

Lee, Anna (n.d.) 'Small victories in the kitchen', *Rat Wars* <www.anysite.com/ members/~annalee/ratwars/kitchen.html> Accessed: 12 March 2012.

A date when it was first written or first put on the web is provided – it is clear that the document has not been updated since and is unlikely to be updated

Lee, Anna (2010) 'Small victories in the kitchen', *Rat Wars* <www.anysite.com/ members/~annalee/ratwars/kitchen.html>.

A date when it was first written or first put on the web is provided – it has been updated since and the date of last updating is provided

Lee, Anna (2010) 'Small victories in the kitchen', *Rat Wars* <www.anysite.com/ members/~annalee/ratwars/kitchen.html> Updated: 10 September 2011.

A date when it was first written or first put on the web is provided – it appears to have been updated since but the date of last updating is not provided

Lee, Anna (2010) 'Small victories in the kitchen', *Rat Wars* <www.anysite.com/ members/~annalee/ratwars/kitchen.html> Accessed: 12 March 2012.

There will be times when you need to cite an entire website or blog, rather than a single post or web page. One legitimate option is simply to mention it in the text of your essay or article and provide the URL: '...this is a feature of the Guardian website (www.guardian.co.uk)', for example. If you need to cite it formally, just provide the name and give the URL for the home page of the website or blog. If the website or blog is an ongoing work, you might cite the year it began and the current year, as in the example below:

Lee, Anna (2007–12) *Rat Wars* <www.anysite.com/members/~annalee/ratwars> Accessed: 12 March 2012.

Sometimes you will need to make reference to the website of an organization, a source for which there is no close print equivalent. In this case, the date the organization first made the website available online is really only of historical interest, because they have an ongoing presence online and you can omit dates entirely. By contrast, a blog or personal website may only last for a year or two. If you need to list websites in your bibliography, as opposed to individual web pages, one option is to list them separately from other sources, as you might list newspapers or archive collections you have used extensively. You can omit dates entirely, as in the example below:

Organization for Economic Development <www.oecd.org>

Dealing with page numbers

In many disciplines you are expected to cite a page number when you make reference to a particular sentence or paragraph in a print document so the reader can find it easily. Giving page numbers for web documents presents some difficulties. If the document is in pdf format, where all of the pages are clearly numbered, there's no problem. But a web page that is seven pages long on your printer could easily be five or nine pages long when printed out on another printer with different settings. One way around this problem is to give the total number of pages in the document, citing it as '2 of 7', for example. This gives a clear indication of which part of the document the quote appears in, even to someone whose printer is set up differently or who is viewing it through their browser. In some types of print documents, such as parliamentary debates or legal documents, it is established practice for paragraphs to be numbered. You cite the paragraph rather than the page number. Where a web document is numbered by paragraph, you can cite these rather than page numbers. Finally, bearing in mind that the central concern here is to be able to locate the original, one of the most effective ways for a reader to locate a quote in a web page is to view the page on their browser and use 'Find' to locate the quote. This fact renders the citing of web page numbers redundant when a quote is involved.

Citing email messages, text messages and online posts

In many cases you can simply mention an email message in your essay or article without formally citing it, referring to 'an email message from [*insert name*] to the author on 12 January 2012', for example. Since a personal message cannot be accessed by those reading the article, there is no need to give the kind of information that would allow a reader to retrieve it and it is enough to provide the date and the name of the author. The same applies to text messages or Facebook posts. If it is a private message or one intended for a strictly limited audience, then you should ask permission before you quote it or cite it at all. If you do need to formally cite an email message or a post to a social network, one that has been distributed publicly, you will find that they are a lot simpler to cite than web documents, requiring minimal detective work. The author is usually the person or organization that sent the message. If the email address is publicly associated with the message (for example, if it was sent out on a public mailing list or if it is available on a website or in a public archive), you can give the email address in the citation. The date is usually the date it was first sent or posted online and the title is the subject heading or an obvious title at the beginning of the message. For email messages, the equivalent of 'site' is the discussion list or mailing list that the message came from – if it came from a list. If it is unclear from the name of the list that it is an email list, put the mailing address for the list after its name, just to make this clear. For posts to social networks, the network is the equivalent of 'site'. If an email is archived on the web, you can also give the URL to allow people to locate the original easily.

Below is a citation for an imaginary email message sent to Quitsmoking-L discussion list.

Mulcahy, Dara (2011) <dara@mulcahynet.ie> 'Giving up cigarettes in Belfast', *Quitsmoking-L*. 28 December 2011 <www.quitsmoking.ie/list/message 432.html>.

Citing discussion group posts

You cite these in much the same way that you cite email messages. Author, date and title are all straightforward enough, while the group the message is posted to is the equivalent of the site.

Mulcahy, Dara (2011) <dara@mulcahynet.ie> 'Giving up cigarettes in Belfast', *soc.smoking.ireland*. 28 December 2011.

Citing blog comments

As with email messages, these can often simply be mentioned in passing: '... in a comment on 17 September on the Smoking Ireland Blog (smoking.irlblog. com)', for example. If an individual comment is so significant that it is essential to include it in the bibliography, you can use the format below:

Mulcahy, Dara (2011) comment on Niamh Quinn, 'Giving up again'. *Smoking Ireland Blog*, 4 February 2011, <smoking.irlblog.com/Quinn/2011/02/again. html> 20 February 2011.

Citing photographs

Printed photographs often belong to collections and are cited as such. If an online photograph belongs to a wider collection online, include the name of that collection in the citation. If it is not, then simply omit this element. The example below cites a photograph that does belong to a wider collection identified as such by the photographer. Ideally, you should provide a URL that will lead directly to the photograph. If a photograph is embedded in a web page and you can't provide a direct link to it, provide the URL for the page.

Lee, Anna (2007) 'Footprints in grease' [Photograph]. Kitchen scenes <www. flickr.com/photos/annalee/130794732>.

Exercises

Exercise 1: Classification

Do a quick search on a keyword search engine such as Google, Yahoo or Bing on a topic that generates controversy and debate. It does not have to be connected to your research topic. You might choose a topic such as 'assisted suicide', or 'insurgency'.

1 Quickly classify the first five hits and briefly explain why you have classified them in this way, describing the information that was crucial in making your judgement. If all five belong to the same category, continue into the next five hits to ensure that your answer deals with hits from at least two different categories.

Exercise 2: Evaluation

Choose two of the web pages you classified in the first exercise, making sure that they belong to two different categories.

1 Evaluate both of them for authority, accuracy, objectivity and currency, according to the guidelines suggested above.
2 Which evaluation questions proved most useful in assessing these web pages?

Exercise 3: Citing web pages

1 Cite the two web pages evaluated in the previous exercise.

Exercise 4: Citing a blog entry

Use a blog search engine such as Google Blog Search or Technorati to identify a blog entry on a topic that generates controversy and debate.

1 Cite the entry, and cite the blog the entry was posted to.

Exercise 5: Citing a public message or post

1 Cite an email you have received from a mailing list or a public post to a social networking site such as Facebook or Google Plus.

Exercise 7: Citing photographs

1 Cite a photograph you have identified through the image search of a major search engine such as Google, Yahoo or Bing.
2 Cite a photograph you have identified through a photo-sharing site such as Flickr, Webshots or Pbase.

NINE

Beyond searching: networks, research management and online research

Previous chapters have focused on searching and understanding online resources. This chapter goes beyond searching to discuss the new online research networks which are becoming an increasingly important part of academic life. It also outlines effective approaches to using the research management software that has become available during the past few years and which provides new ways to organize the vast literatures that are now accessible to us. Finally, the chapter looks at one of the fastest growing areas of academic research, the study of the way in which the Internet is bound up with deep changes in the character of politics and society. New technologies are facilitating dramatic changes in the character of public protest, rebellion, war and political participation as well as deep changes in the way in which we interact with one another in our daily lives. Rather than simply using the Internet as a tool for finding information about the 'real world', more and more researchers and scholars are now investigating what we do online and how it is related to our offline activities, using the Internet to gather new data. We outline the innovative research methods these researchers are currently developing.

Research networks and research support

Postgraduate students and academic researchers have always benefited from contact with others around them in the same position, particularly from contact with those working on related topics. This is particularly important for students working on a thesis or dissertation. People working in the same physical location remain a key source of support, but online access to the experience and knowledge of others in the same position is an increasingly important supplement to this. This section outlines some of the key online resources and strategies for building your network of research contacts and drawing on the knowledge and support of others to advance your own work.

Social networks

A key difficulty with some of the most popular social networking sites, Facebook and Google Plus chief among them, is the fact that they blur the boundaries between different aspects of your life and work. Friends and family might rightly get irritated if you constantly post material from your research project and notices about academic events to a social networking site. Equally, there are aspects of your personal and family life that you might well be unhappy sharing with fellow-researchers and random professional contacts. There are mechanisms for managing these problems in services such as Facebook where you can group people using the 'lists' feature, but they require more effort than many people are willing to expend. The use of 'Circles' in Google Plus addresses this problem by making it easy to separate different categories of people, but there are also a number of alternative social networks catering specifically to postgraduate students and academic researchers. Most of these networks allow you to cross-link between them, so you can post content simultaneously to several social networks.

Academia.edu

Billed as 'Facebook for academics', this social network is focused on distributing research papers and publications and building connections to, and mutual awareness of, people working in closely related areas. You can select multiple 'research interests' to associate with your profile. The number of people associated with each topic is displayed, giving you a sense of the volume of work in different subject areas. Some of the subject areas are very specialized indeed and you can devise new 'research interests' of your own and see if anyone else signs up. You can list conference presentations, papers or publications of your own, and other members of academia.edu who choose to 'follow' you will be notified whenever you list new material. You can also post the full text of the papers. For many researchers

Figure 9.1 Academia.edu image

this provides a way to increase awareness of their work and increase the chances that other academics will cite them and use their work. You can similarly 'follow' other people. It may make sense to 'follow' a few of the key writers in your field and to follow other PhD candidates working in the area (if you are doing a PhD). This very global service also provides a way to stay up to date with the work that is going on in your institution, something that we sometimes neglect to do as we roam far and wide online. Just 'follow' colleagues in your own department or school to stay up to date with the work that's going on all around you.

ResearchGate (www.researchgate.net/)

This is a larger and longer-established social network for academics but it appears to be much more strongly focused on the natural sciences than **academia.edu**.

Figure 9.2 ResearchGate image

Blogs

Postgraduate students – Grad students in US terminology – are among the most intensive users of social networking tools and the most active participants in online discussion. Substantial numbers of them, in the USA in particular, have set up personal blogs (short for 'web log') that often include useful advice on a wide range of issues involved in writing a thesis or dissertation. These blogs can be particularly useful in providing information on the latest software and research resources being used by these students. They are very uneven in their quality and much advice does not travel very well beyond national boundaries because the educational systems vary so widely, but it is well worth exploring the Blogosphere to see if there are one or two useful blogs by postgraduate students in your area. *The Thesis Whisperer* (**thethesiswhisperer.wordpress.com**) provides a good example with a UK focus, and provides links to a large number of other PhD-related blogs.

To find advice on research organization software from PhD students, for example, combine search terms like **"phd student"** or **phd** with the name of the package you want to know about: **phd evernote** or **"phd student" mendeley** for example. It is worth searching in specialized blog search engines (**technorati.com** or **blogs.google.com**) as well as regular search engines such as Google,

Yahoo and Bing. Once you have found one good blog in your area you can follow the links on the blogroll to identify others, in much the same way that you follow references from a key text.

One of the best ways to identify some key blogs in your area is through the hundreds of 'Top Ten' lists (**www.blogs.com/topten/**) at Blogs.com. Use broad search terms to search the massive list on this page using the 'find' search box on your browser. A lot of the lists have been carefully compiled by individuals with specialized expertise, many of them academics.

Many academic blogs provide extensive advice to research students on a wide range of issues. For example, **orgtheory.net**, provides an extensive set of 'grad skool rulz' for PhD students (**orgtheory.wordpress.com/grad-skool-rulz**) that are useful and relevant well beyond the US context to which they primarily relate. The 'rulz' also provide an insight into the nature of postgraduate research in the US for those outside that system.

Creating a blog

It is now a simple matter for anyone to set up a blog in the space of 10–15 minutes through one of the big popular blogging services such as **Blogger.com, Wordpress. com** or **Blogspot.com**. As the name suggests, blogs were originally characterized as a method of 'posting' regularly updated information but they have now become the default option for anyone setting up a personal website because they are so easy to use and so versatile. Researchers use blogs to post links to web pages or images or news stories or academic articles that have grabbed their attention. In addition to 'posting', you can also create 'pages' on your blog where you can post your CV or information about your research interests, activities or publications. Academics and PhD students create blogs in order to provide a showcase for their work and their interests that other researchers will come across if they do a search on their name. Think of it as a CV that will come to the top of any search on your name.

Other resources

Vitae (**www.vitae.ac.uk**) Established specifically to cater for PhD students and academic research staff in the UK, this academic service provides a range of resources, including advice on 'Managing your research project' (**www.vitae. ac.uk/researchers/1220/Managing-your-research-project.html**).

H-Grad (**www.h-net.org/~grad/**) This is an email list open to postgraduate students everywhere. It deals with a range of issues, including teaching, time management, research concerns, computer programs, choosing an adviser, and job-seeking. Some of the material is of universal interest but the heavy American emphasis means that students

Figure 9.3 Vitae image

outside the USA will find that much of it is of limited value. The website provides links to related resources. Members can search the archives of messages.

JISCmail lists (**www.jiscmail.ac.uk**) As the UK's academic mailing list service, this includes a wide range of mailing lists catering specifically for postgraduate students in individual subject areas.

Postgraduate Forum (**www.postgraduateforum.com**) This has a huge collection of discussion lists for postgraduate students across the world. A search on the title of a reference management package such as EndNote, Zotero or Mendeley brings up advice and links to other sources of information on the topic.

Organizing your research

There is a lot to be said for simple, low-tech approaches to organizing your research. Some of the most productive and celebrated writers and researchers get by without any of the elaborate tools that have become available in recent years. They type their notes up in Word or a similar word-processing package and enter their references into their articles and essays themselves. The argument that getting to grips with rapidly-changing software solutions swallows up as much time as it saves has much to commend it. It can be especially wasteful to invest time in working with a new service or product that is full of glitches that ultimately cancel out the time-saving features it offers. You may find that you have invested a lot of time in a service that never irons out those teething problems and then declines and disappears. This is the perennial problem of the 'early adopter', those who are the first to incorporate new technologies and services into their lives. Those who shun the latest technological innovation derive the considerable benefit of avoiding a major diversion from their intense focus on their research topic. Even the most heavily-used, long-lived and popular reference management packages are still dogged by glitches and weaknesses. The promise of an almost magically seamless workflow is never quite realized. There always seems to be some problem that requires you to go in and edit things yourself.

That said, developments during the past three to four years have seen a giant leap forward in the capabilities and reliability of such services. One of the most important developments is the synchronization of services across a range of computers and electronic devices. Virtually all of the research management packages now allow you to synchronize your information between all of the computers you use, an online version of the service and portable electronic devices including iPhones, Blackberries and tablets such as the iPad. You add a reference or some research notes online, or on your laptop, and they are automatically available on all of your devices.

Even if you don't wish to use the full range of capabilities in these services, it is a simple matter to learn how to use them in a low-tech way that requires little investment of time on your part but will speed up certain key tasks considerably.

The original core function of the reference management packages such as EndNote, ProCite or Reference Manager was to make it easy for you to add references and a bibliography to your essay or article. You export references from a library catalogue or a big database of articles such as Google Scholar, Scopus, ISI Web of Knowledge or the many others dealt with in Chapters 3 and 4.

You import them into your reference management package and you can then display them according to the citation system you are using. Increasingly, exported references are automatically imported into reference management packages, removing one step from the sequence. The main advantage of importing from databases is that you never have to type out the full citation details yourself. If you take references directly from Google Scholar, you will have the slightly frustrating experience of having to export and then import references one at a time, slowing down the process, although services such as Mendeley now make it much easier to import several references from Scholar at once. One great advantage of using the big services such as Worldcat or your library catalogue (for books), Scopus or ISI Web of Knowledge is that you can import large

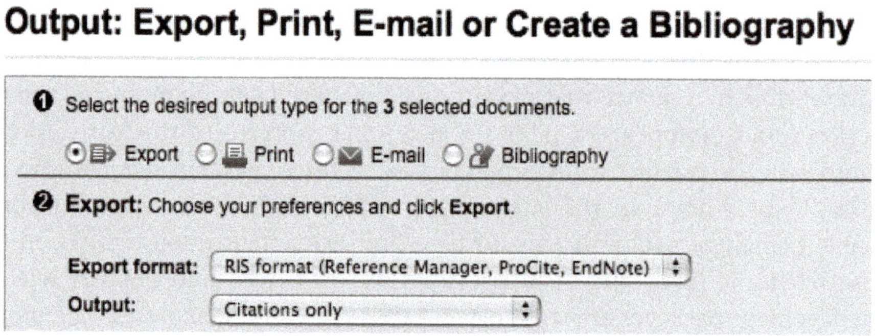

Output: Export, Print, E-mail or Create a Bibliography

❶ Select the desired output type for the **3** selected documents.

⦿ ▣⏵ Export   ○ 🖨 Print   ○ ✉ E-mail   ○ 📖 Bibliography

❷ **Export:** Choose your preferences and click **Export**.

Export format: | RIS format (Reference Manager, ProCite, EndNote) ⬍ |

Output: | Citations only ⬍ |

Figure 9.4   Reference export options in Scopus

Figure 9.5   Reference export options in ISI Web of Knowledge

numbers of references together with a single click. You can identify references over several different searches, saving them to your account each time: these services allow you to register for free for a personal account if your institution is subscribed. After several such searches you can export all of the results together and import them into your reference management package in one batch.

Once you have imported the references to EndNote or RefWorks or another package, you can take a very simple low-tech approach to using the service if you don't want to spend any time learning how to use it. Simply preview a reference in the citation format you are using, then copy and paste it into your essay or article. You don't have to get to grips with any of the instructions on importing references into Word documents and creating bibliographies but you will still save yourself a considerable amount of time.

Note that all of the databases are imperfect and that references are frequently imported with some data missing. If you import from Google Scholar, ISI Web of Knowledge or Scopus, for example, you will find that you only have the first initials of authors even though many citation styles in the humanities and social sciences require you to provide the full name. JSTOR, a service which includes a high proportion of history journals, supplies the full names with downloaded references because most citation styles in history require them. You will sometimes find that you don't have the page details for articles, or the place of publication or that you have an over-elaborate version of the publisher's name that you should cut back. Some citation styles insist on capitals for every word in a book or article title while others insist on lower case for all but the first word. If you make sure your references conform to the latter format, you give yourself added flexibility as the software will automatically capitalize for certain styles but won't replace capitals with lower-case letters. Don't be tempted to edit every reference as you import, unless you are sure you will be using it. It can be quite time-consuming. Instead you should check references for accuracy and correct them only when you know you need to use them, just before inserting them in your essay or article or book. You should also make sure you always back up, or make a copy of, these 'libraries', particularly if you store all your research notes in them.

Reference management and research management services also provide various versions of a 'Cite-while-you-write' feature. This allows you to insert correctly formatted references into a Word document as you write. This is well worth doing if you are prepared to deal with the glitches that have still not been ironed out in the software. If you are writing for publication, one of the greatest advantages of these packages is that you can choose a different citation style for your document with a single click if it is rejected by one journal and you want to submit to another journal with a different citation style.

One of the ongoing problems with reference management packages is that it can be difficult to identify the correct style for the journal you are planning to submit to from the thousands of styles provided. There is a heavy focus on journals in the natural sciences, but in the social sciences and humanities you are much less likely to find a style that is aimed specifically at the journal you wish to submit to. Even if the same style is used by a different journal that is covered, it is not always easy to discover this.

Notes, quotes and references

In recent years the existing reference management software packages have been joined by services that aim to manage references and more besides. Research management services such as Zotero and Mendeley are still reference management systems at their core but they provide added features for managing your reading, your personal library of books and articles, and your research notes. This in turn has prompted the existing providers, such as EndNote, to expand the features on their services in order to compete. As a result, many reference management packages are in the process of mutating into research management tools.

These tools are primarily aimed at helping you to organize your reading rather than to organize any research data you might have. Because of the features that allow you to search the full text of documents and to add research notes to these documents, however, they can also be useful for organizing text-based primary data, including transcripts of interviews or focus groups, or copies of archival documents or newspaper stories or web pages.

A key feature of the current batch of services is that they allow you to manage three different but connected sets of information: the full text of readings, citation details for those readings, and your notes on those readings, including text that you might want to quote and cite in your own work. When you come to incorporate material from these readings into your own work, you have all three of these elements easily to hand. You can work your notes into your essay or article as well as scanning the original text for quotes you have highlighted. You can group readings into folders or groups so that all of the materials you plan to refer to in your current project or chapter are gathered together and are easy to search as a kind of little specialized collection that combines your notes and the full text of the readings. As you fold your notes into your own work, you insert the related references. Your own work constitutes a fourth key element that is integrated with the other three elements through the 'Cite-as-you-write' features offered by some of these services. If you have pdf files of book chapters or books, they can also be easily integrated into these services.

Reference management software: focus on EndNote

EndNote, ProCite and *Reference Manager* are perhaps the most popular and long-established subscription reference management packages used by scholars in the social sciences and humanities. Which of these you use (if any) may well be determined by the choices made by your university or library on which of these to subscribe to. I deal here in detail with one of them, to illustrate the kinds of features available in these long-established services. Along with ProCite and Reference Manager, EndNote has in recent years been playing catch-up with its free online competitors. EndNote's greatest strength is the fact that it retains its original focus on references. This ensures that it has one of the largest collections of citation styles – over 3,000 of them. It is also extremely well integrated with Word through its 'Cite-while-you-write' feature. EndNote is owned by the same corporation that owns ISI Web of Knowledge and the two services are integrated to a certain degree. You can export references from ISI Web of Knowledge to EndNote with a single click. EndNote allows you to create multiple 'libraries' but it is simplest to build a single library and use 'groups' to organize your references within the library. You can share groups online with colleagues and collaborators through EndNote's online presence, *EndNote Web*.

Importing references and full text

All of the online databases and library catalogues give you the option to export references in a form suitable for EndNote and you can export and then import large numbers of references to EndNote in one go. You can then download the individual pdf files with the full text of these items and drag them into the 'File attachments' fields of the records for each item. Alternatively, you can search a wide variety of these databases (but not all of them by any means) directly through EndNote's 'Online search' option. This cuts out the 'import' step as search results are automatically imported to EndNote.

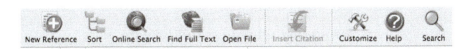

Figure 9.6 EndNote toolbar image

The 'Find Full Text' feature is intended to allow you to find and import a large number of pdf files with a single click but it does not yet work very effectively. You select references in your EndNote library and then click on the 'Find Full Text' button to tell EndNote to look online for the full-text pdf files for these references. If EndNote locates a pdf, it will insert a pdf icon in the 'File attachments' field of the reference in your library and store the pdf in the 'data' folder associated with your EndNote library.

The most recent versions of EndNote also allow you to import multiple pdf files into EndNote from your own computer. EndNote automatically extracts citation data from them and adds them to your reference library, just as newer services like Mendeley do. The pdf is automatically attached to the reference. Where EndNote can't extract citation data, it attaches the pdf file to an empty citation record and allows you to fill in the details yourself. This means you don't need to download references at all. Instead, download multiple pdfs from online databases, put them all together in a folder on your own computer and then import them into EndNote.

Research notes

You can enter your own notes into the *Research Notes* field of each reference. You can then do a search of EndNote limited to the research notes or a combined search of the research notes and the full text of attachments (pdf files). If you regularly use the research notes feature, it can be useful to change the preferences for 'display fields' to display research notes in the main window alongside references. EndNote 'shared groups' on EndNoteWeb allows you to share selected references, including your research notes, with colleagues. The research notes features in EndNote are less sophisticated than those in the new wave of dedicated research management services dealt with below.

Bibliographies

To quickly generate a bibliography, create a group in EndNote and then drag the references you want to use into the group. Make sure you have chosen the citation style you want to use and make sure they are sorted alphabetically. Then select them all and choose **Edit - Copy Formatted** to copy them. Paste the copied references into any document to create a bibliography. Alternatively, select **Export** from the **File** menu to create the bibliography in a text file.

Formatted references in EndNote

You will often find you want to modify the references you insert in a Word document by, for example, adding a page reference. If you add the page number to the reference in Word by typing it in, you interfere with the formatting and may find that the additional information disappears when you save the document. Instead you have to add the page numbers as a 'suffix' in EndNote. The key thing to remember is to change the citation details in your reference management software and, if necessary, insert the reference again. Don't edit the formatted reference directly.

There are advantages to leaving the EndNote references in your Word document unformatted until the document is finished. It makes the document a lot smaller because it doesn't add the hidden 'field codes' associated with each reference. Choose the option to 'Unformat Citation(s)' or 'Convert to Unformatted Citations'. A bibliography will not be added until you format the citations. When you are ready to submit the essay or article, format the references and add the bibliography by selecting 'Format Bibliography' or 'Update Citations and Bibliography'.

Most publishers want a 'clean copy' of your document without all the *hidden* EndNote field codes but retaining all of the correctly formatted citations. **Remove Field Codes** or **Convert Citations and Bibliography** → **Convert to Plain Text** to create a clean copy that leaves the original document intact. If you subsequently submit it to a different journal that uses a different citation system you can go back and change the formatting in the original document with a single click.

Research organization services: focus on Mendeley

The beauty of Mendeley (**www.mendeley.com**) is that it integrates citation information, the full text of articles and your notes and notations on the texts you are reading. You can begin using Mendeley and store substantial amounts of material there without paying, but you have to pay to store more than the permitted amount. If you genuinely begin to use this as the spine of your research work, it seems likely that you will need to store more data than is allocated to non-paying users. If you become dependent on the service and it becomes more popular, there is always the risk that they will change the payment model and you will need to become a paying subscriber to continue using it at all.

One of the best features of Mendeley is that it allows you to do a search of the full text of the documents in your collection. It allows you to filter the results by author, journal or tag and arrange them according to the date when you added them to your library, to bring the most recent to the front. If you systematically add all of the texts you use in your research to Mendeley, you effectively create a searchable personal library. The resultant collection is so specific to your own research that you can get valuable and useful results by searching on simple search terms. You can turn up half-remembered quotes or details by entering one

Figure 9.7 Mendeley image

or two common words from the quote. A search on common words that would generate millions of results out on the open Web will often be sufficient to locate a crucial piece of information in a personal collection of this kind. Searching in this collection for the name of an individual, or an event or a concept, will turn up all of the discussions in which they have been mentioned. This is potentially an extremely valuable resource in its own right.

Another striking feature of Mendeley is the way in which it is integrated with a variety of other citation and reference management services. If you already use CiteULike or Zotero (discussed below), you can synchronize them with Mendeley and every time you add a reference to either of these services it will also be added to Mendeley. If you are already using EndNote, RefWorks or Reference Manager, you can import all of your references from these packages into Mendeley.

You can arrange your documents in folders as well as tagging them. To get easy access to all of the articles and books that relate to the essay or article or PhD chapter you are currently writing, just tag them all with a tag specific to that project. You can share and synchronize all or part of your library with colleagues to create a shared library for a particular project in which you can view comments and annotations on the full text of pdf files by all users.

Importing references and full text

The ease with which you can import references together with the full text of documents into Mendeley is extremely impressive, when it works. There are still glitches. In the case of Google Scholar, for example, you can set search preferences so that the search results page shows a hundred results. Clicking 'Import to Mendeley' on your browser then generates a pop up page which allows you to import both references and full text (where available) for any of these hundred search results.

You can import citation details together with full text directly from a huge number of databases of books and articles, including Google Scholar, JStor, ISI Web of Knowledge, ScienceDirect, Wiley Online Library and Amazon, as well as importing web pages and their citation details and archiving copies of those web pages.

Import documents to Mendeley

From: http://scholar.google.com/scholar?hl=en&num=100&q=territoriality+machiavelli+power&btnG=Search&
as_sdt=0%2C5&as_ylo=&as_vis=0

⊕ Import   **Racism, Territoriality and Ethnocentricity**
Feuchtwang, S (1990)
i Alrick X & Stephan Feuchtwang (red.), Antiracist ...

⊕ Import   **Machiavelli in machina: Or politics among hexagons**
(1977)
Problems of world modeling

⊕ Import   **Towards a bio-territorial conception of power: Territory, population, and environmental**
narratives in Palestine and Israel
Alatout, S (2006)
Political Geography

Figure 9.8   Mendeley scholar image

You can choose from more than 1,000 citation styles, not quite the same range of choice available in EndNote, although the number will undoubtedly increase. In addition, the facilites to integrate references with Word and other word-processing packages through Mendeley's 'Generate citations as you write' plug-ins are not quite as well developed as in EndNote.

Drag and drop pdfs into Mendeley and it automatically extracts citation data and adds the full text to its searchable database, even for scanned pdfs. This applies to pdfs of books and book chapters as well as to articles. It then checks your pdfs against the big databases and pulls in any additional citation information that is available.

Research notes

Research notes sometimes seem like an afterthought in traditional reference management services such as EndNote but in Mendeley they take centre stage, a fact reflected in the display window, where research notes and annotations are given as much space as the full text of documents. You can write research notes, highlight text, and attach sticky notes with comments to pdf files and then share these annotated pdfs with colleagues. You can also export these annotated pdfs.

Other Research management services

Zotero (www.zotero.org)

Zotero was the original online research management service, free to all and developed collaboratively as an open source service. It pioneered many of the features now available in other services such as Mendeley, including archiving web pages and allowing you to annotate texts in your library and write research notes. You can tag items and organize them into collections and you can share your library with others online.

Like Mendeley, it is not as well integrated with word-processing packages or as focused on providing vast numbers of citation styles as are the dedicated reference management services such as EndNote. But on the plus side it makes it very easy to import references and the full text of files online through a Zotero button on your browser. It also permits you to do a search of the full text of documents in your library.

Figure 9.9   Zotero image

Sente (www.thirdstreetsoftware.com)

A very sophisticated reference management package only available for MacOSX and iPad. It has many of the desirable features we see in Mendeley and the most recent versions of EndNote, allowing you to annotate pdfs and enter your own research notes.

Downloads of both references and pdfs from online databases and web pages are quick and easy. Drag pdfs into Sente and it will extract citation information. Enter an identifying code, such as an ISBN for a book or a DOI (a unique identifying code for an online article), and it will attempt to retrieve full citation details online.

CiteULike (www.CiteULike.com)

This free online service allows you to easily import references, add extensive notes to them and share these with other users of CiteULike. You can also do a search of the full text of all of the pdfs that you add to your library. One of the features that sets it apart from most other reference management services is the emphasis on networking and connecting to others. You can see who else is reading the articles you are reading, and who has added any given item to their

Figure 9.10   CiteULike image

library and you can share articles on social networking sites such as Facebook. It provides a way to see what people who are working in your area are reading. The list put together by an established expert on table-manners in eighteenth-century France, or a PhD student working on the topic, constitutes a kind of specialized, personalized bibliography that may be extremely useful to someone else who is beginning to work in the area. You use tags to group articles together. It is not well integrated with word-processing software but you can 'export' your library easily enough, then import it to a package like EndNote that is well integrated with Word. You can join 'groups' dedicated to gathering together literature on a particular topic or associated with a particular project or reading group, can give people the unique URL of your personal CiteULike page so they can see what you are reading.

EverNote (www.evernote.com)

Aimed at allowing you to store a wide range of materials, this is not particularly strong on organization or structure. Its great strength is flexibility. As with other services, you can use it both online and on your various computers and electronic devices and synchronize the content on all of these. As well as capturing web pages and saving documents and pdfs, you can add images and audio files. One distinctive feature is the OCR (Optical Character Recognition) capacity that allows you to extend your full-text search to written notes and scanned texts that you include in EverNote. You can gather together related materials in 'Notebooks' and do a search that searches your notes as well as the text of this wide range of materials.

Figure 9.11 EverNote image

Figure 9.12 Dropbox image

Dropbox (www.dropbox.com)

Strictly speaking, this is not a research management tool but it performs one simple task that is of value to any researcher in managing their work. It creates a 'dropbox' folder on your various computers and electronic devices as well as allowing you online access to this folder, and it synchronizes the contents of this folder at all of these locations. Drag a file to the dropbox folder on any of the devices you use and it is available to you on all of these devices and is also available to you online.

Internet research methods

The new technologies have provided us with a range of powerful tools for gathering information that social scientists have always collected. Perhaps the most notable of these are the new online survey systems that allow us to gather data from respondents across the globe cheaply and quickly. In addition to new systems based on established research practices and used for asking familiar questions, new technologies such as the big search engines and social networks are generating large quantities of novel kinds of data. These data provide information about the way in which people interact and the way in which their interests vary geographically and shift over time. These are new kinds of information about new kinds of activities but they are being deployed very effectively to address some of the most long-standing and significant debates in the social sciences. While both of these developments provide us with new ways of learning about long-standing problems and patterns, the Internet has also generated deep shifts in the nature of the social and produced new phenomena that we are only just beginning to understand. A new generation of online social scientists is concerned not only to use new technologies to understand social patterns, but also to understand the significance of new forms of activity and of the increasingly rapid pace of social change.

To take just one example, the new technologies have facilitated a deep transformation in the nature of warfare. The proliferation of online materials generated by soldiers on the front lines of contemporary wars runs parallel with intensely hostile online interaction between civilians who confront each other from their widely-separated locations on the respective 'home fronts'. Alongside this, new battlefield technologies allow remote control of operations and weapons from distant command sites on the other side of the globe. Military personnel can view, identify and kill their human targets on screens many thousands of miles from the actual site of killing, while the use of electronic barriers and surveillance are now central to military strategies for controlling occupied territories. The changes facilitated by new information technologies in this one crucial aspect of human interaction alone are so swift and sweeping that we have barely begun to understand their consequences for warfare and for global society.

The *Sage Handbook of Online Research Methods* (Fielding et al., 2008) covers a wide range of issues in online research, from ethics and legal issues to problems with data collection. It also surveys the state of debate on a range of online research tools and methods. AOIR, the Association of Internet Researchers (**www.aoir.org**) is the main professional association for those researching online activity and using online research tools. Influential books and articles on Internet research methods include Jones (1998); Kaye and Johnson (1999); Kollock and Smith (1999); Hine (2000, 2005); Mann and Stewart (2000); Nesbary (2000); and Best and Krueger (2004). The AOIR wiki provides a list of research centres that are focused on the relationship between society and the new technologies (**wiki.aoir.org/index.php?title=Research_Centers**). There is also a huge volume of research work taking place beyond those centres. Much of this work is published in mainstream journals in the social sciences and humanities but there are also a number of key journals devoted entirely to publishing this kind of work, including: *New Media and Society*: *Information, Communication and Society;* and *The Information Society*.

Online surveys

SurveyGizmo and Survey Monkey are two of the best-known and most heavily-used online survey systems. The AOIR wiki page on 'Online surveys' (**wiki.aoir.org/index.php?title=Online_Surveys**) provides information on these and several other online survey systems and links to several guides to online surveys. There are certain drawbacks to online surveys, not least of them the danger of low response rates and the difficulty of gathering a representative sample. A variety of methods have been developed to allow researchers to work their way around these problems.

Online ethnography

Some online ethnographies rely entirely on observation of online interaction between members of a virtual community or observation of specific kinds of sites and networks. Some ethnographers argue strongly for the importance of participation by the researcher, in emulation of the traditional ethnographic practice in which researchers immerse themselves in the cultures and communities they study and understand them from within. Researchers from Sherry Turkle (1995) onwards have emphasized that online interaction cannot be understood in isolation from the physical contexts in which participants are located and the 'real-world' social networks in which they are embedded. Online interaction and offline contexts have to be understood together, as they are in the recent ethnographic literature surveyed by Leander and McKim (2003: 223), which 'has begun to document how online and offline practices and spaces are co-constituted, hybridized, and embedded within one another'.

Online interviews

Researchers have begun to use online interviews as a way of reaching people who would otherwise be inaccessible, conducting synchronous online interviews through online chat and 'asynchronous' interviews by email. The latter are useful because respondents have a chance to think about the question and put together a more considered reply. However, the lack of cues as to an interviewee's mood or tone means that the interviewer gets far less information about interviewee's responses than they would in a face-to-face interview. It is much more difficult to assess whether the interviewee is uncomfortable with a question or being evasive and it is difficult to establish the sense of personal connection on which trust is built and which encourages an interviewee to speak candidly. New audio and video technologies including *Skype* make it much less expensive and much simpler to conduct online interviews that include voice and video.

Online focus groups

To create an online focus group, selected participants are invited to log on together to conferencing software at a specific time and take part in an online discussion on the topic, guided by a moderator. New facilities for easy video-conferencing through social networks such as Google Plus are expanding the possibilities for conducting online focus groups that include video. As with all online interaction, the absence of a range of cues to people's mood and attitude that are available when people are in the same location mean that the results from an online focus group are likely to differ quite significantly from the results that emerge when people are gathered together in a room.

Web-based experiments

Experiments conducted over the Internet have been relatively widely used in psychology and linguistics. They might involve, for example, asking people to answer questions before and after viewing a piece of footage or performing a task online.

New forms of data

As a by-product of their primary functions, Google and Facebook generate huge volumes of data that can help us to understand much more than the way in which people use these services. For example, one study used publicly-available information from Facebook accounts to trace the development of relationships between new students at a US university. The results were used to assess the relative importance of nationality, ethnic background, everyday contact, residence, social class and race in influencing whether students developed closer relationships (Wimmer and Lewis, 2010).

Google Correlate (**correlate.googlelabs.com**) This allows you to create charts that show how the popularity of particular search terms varies over time, and maps that indicate how their popularity varies between US states. Given that Google's data covers the entire globe and that search patterns can be analyzed according to the precise location of individual computers, there is potential for analyzing this data in much more sophisticated ways to track variation within cities and neighbourhoods as well as between regions and countries. It opens up immense possibilities for social scientists and humanities scholars.

Google Trends (**www.google.com/trends**) This tracks both search patterns and news trends over time, allowing us to map the rise and fall of popular and media interest in particular search terms.

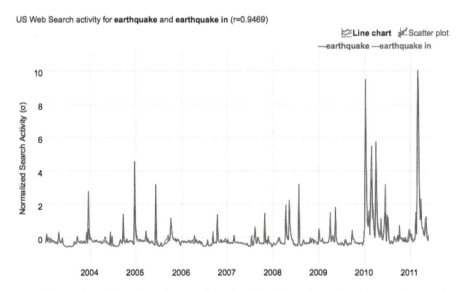

Figure 9.13 Chart from Google Correlate showing the spike in Google searches on the word 'earthquake' after major earthquakes in Haiti in January 2010 and New Zealand and Japan in early 2011

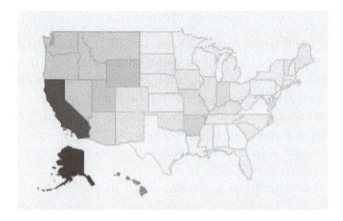

Figure 9.14 Map from Google Correlate showing that US searches on the term 'earthquake' are most common in states bordering the Pacific ocean

New research fields

The rapid changes in social interaction facilitated by the new technologies has generated new fields of research in recent years. One of the fastest-growing fields is the academic study of computer games. Computer games have become so central to modern culture that they now present a serious challenge to the dominance of television-viewing as the primary entertainment medium. Online games in particular have very strong interactive dimensions that foster the building of connections and interchange between people who often come from opposite sides of the globe. Political preferences, gender, class and nationality repeatedly burst through into online games. Many academics have focused on interaction in MMORPGs (Massively Multi-player Online Role-Playing Games), such as *World of Warcraft*, which have huge numbers of players across the world and in which interaction is central to the game. *Game Studies* (**www.gamestudies.org**), a cross-disciplinary journal, is the first academic journal dedicated entirely to the study of computer games.

APPENDIX

Academic blogs in the social sciences and the humanities

The list below is dominated by blogs that rely on the collective work of people with a shared interest in the subject area. Virtually all of them provide extensive links to closely-related blogs and provide a good starting point for discovering a wide range of other blogs in the subject area dealt with.

Some of those listed below are the official blogs of professional associations. Among the most common kinds of materials on academic blogs are information and discussion about recent research findings, about research grants and jobs, about key academic resources (especially new resources) and about contemporary public debates related to the subject area. They frequently host discussion and exchange of information on practical issues facing researchers in the discipline. Many of them are used for the distribution of syllabi, reading lists and other teaching materials, for conference announcements and for reporting on research workshops or publicising new research papers.

Anthropology

American Anthropological Association (blog.aaanet.org)
Ethnography.com
Savage Minds: Notes and Queries in Anthropology (savageminds.org)

Archaeology

Cronaca (www.cronaca.com)

Economics

EconLog: Library of Economics and Liberty (econlog.econlib.org)
Economix: explaining the science of everyday life (economix.blogs.nytimes.com)
Marginal Revolution (marginalrevolution.blogs.com)

Geography

Cultural Geography blog (cultcha.blogspot.com)
GIS Lounge (geography.gislounge.com)

History

American Historical Association (blog.historians.org)
The History Blog (www.thehistoryblog.com)
History News Network (www.hnn.us)

Philosophy

Leiter Reports: a philosophy blog (leiterreports.typepad.com)

Politics

Crooked Timber: politics and current affairs (crookedtimber.org)
Public Reason: a blog for political philosophers (publicreason.net)

Psychology

British Psychological Society Research Digest (bps-research-digest.blogspot.com)
Social Psychology Eye (socialpsychologyeye.wordpress.com)

Science, design, literature, current affairs, art

3 Quarks Daily (3quarksdaily.blogs.com)

Sociology

Everyday Sociology (nortonbooks.typepad.com/everydaysociology)
Montclair SocioBlog (montclairsoci.blogspot.com)
Orgtheory.net: Organization theory blog (orgtheory.wordpress.com)
Public Criminology (thesocietypages.org/pubcrim)

Statistics

Social Science Statistics Blog (www.iq.harvard.edu/blog/sss/)

Bibliography

Adams, Douglas (1979) *The Hitchhiker's Guide to the Galaxy.* London: Pan Books.

Agre, Philip E. (1996) 'The art of getting help', *Red Rock Eater News*, 8 October <rre@weber.ucsd.edu>.

Ahrens, Frank (1999) 'The cyber-saga of the "sunscreen" song', *The Washington Post*, 18 March <www.washingtonpost.com/wp-srv/style/features/daily/march99/sunscreen 0318.htm>.

Alexander, Janet E. and Tate, Marsha Ann (1999) *Web Wisdom: How to Evaluate and Create Information Quality on the Web.* Mahwah, NJ/London: Lawrence Erlbaum Associates.

Antelman, Kristin (2004) 'Do open-access articles have a greater research impact?', *College & Research Libraries*, 65 (5): 372–82 <eprints.rclis.org/archive/00002309/>.

Basch, Reva (1996) *Secrets of the Super Net Searchers: The Reflections, Revelations, and Hard-Won Wisdom of 35 of the World's Top Internet Researchers.* Wilton, CT: Pemberton Press.

Basch, Reva (1998) *Researching Online for Dummies.* Foster City, CA: IDG Books Worldwide.

Bauerlein, Mark (2008) *The Dumbest Generation: How the Digital Age Stupefies Young Americans and Jeopardizes Our Future (or, Don't Trust Anyone under 30).* New York: Tarcher.

BBC News (2005) 'Authors sue Google over book plan', *BBC News*, 21 September <news.bbc.co.uk/1/hi/business/4266586.stm>.

Best, Samuel and Krueger, Brian (2004) *Internet Data Collection.* London: Sage.

Calishain, Tara (1998–2006) *ResearchBuzz* <www.researchbuzz.com>.

Carr, Nicholas (2010) *The Shallows: What the Internet is Doing to Our Brains.* New York: W.W. Norton.

Ellis, Judith (1993) *Keeping Archives* (2nd edn). Port Melbourne: Thorpe in association with the Australian Society of Archivists.

Encyclopaedia Britannica (2006) 'Fatally flawed: refuting the recent study on encyclopaedic accuracy by the journal *Nature*' [press release], March.

Feeney, Mary (ed.), National Preservation Office (1999) *Digital Culture: Maximising the Nation's Investment.* London: British Library.

Fielding, Nigel, Lee, Raymond M. and Blank, Grant (2008) *The Sage Handbook of Online Research Methods.* London: Sage.

Giles, Jim (2005) 'Internet encyclopaedias go head to head', *Nature*, 438 (15 December): 900–1.

Goodwin, Danny (2011) 'May 2011 search engine market share from comScore, compete, hitwise', *Search Engine Watch*, 19 June <searchenginewatch.com/article/2080003/May-2011-Search-Engine-Market-Share-from-comScore-Compete-Hitwise>.

Grossman, Wendy (1997) *Net.wars.* New York: New York University Press.

Harley, Diane and Acord, Sophia (2011) *Peer Review in Academic Promotion and Publishing: Its Meaning, Locus, and Future*. Berkeley, CA: Center for Studies in Higher Education, University of California Berkeley <escholarship.org/uc/item/1xv148c8>.

Hine, Christine (2000) *Virtual Ethnography*. London: Sage.

Hine, Christine (ed.) (2005) *Virtual Methods: Issues in Social Research on the Internet*. Oxford: Berg.

Hoff, Jens, Horrocks, Ivan and Tops, Pieter (eds) (2000) *Democratic Governance and New Technology: Technologically Mediated Innovations in Political Practice in Western Europe*. Routledge/ECPR Studies in European Political Science. London/New York: Routledge.

Infopeople (2006) 'Best Search Tools Chart', *Infopeople* <www.infopeople.org/search/chart.html> (last updated: 8 March 2006).

Jackson, Maggie (2009) *Distracted: The Erosion of Attention and the Coming Dark Age*. Amherst, NY: Prometheus Books.

Jacsó, Peter (2005) 'As we may search: comparison of major features of the Web of Science, Scopus, and Google Scholar citation-based and citation-enhanced databases', *Current Science*, 89 (9): 1537–47.

Jacsó, Peter (2011) 'Google Scholar duped and deduped: the aura of "robometrics"', *Online Information Review*, 35 (1):154–60.

Jones, Steve (ed.) (1998) *Doing Internet Research: Critical Issues and Methods for Examining the Net*. London: Sage.

Jones, Steve and Johnson-Yale, Camille (2005) 'Professors online: the Internet's impact on college faculty', *First Monday*, 10 (9) <firstmonday.org/issues/issue10_9/jones/ index. html>.

Jones, Steve and Madden, Mary (2002) *The Internet Goes to College: How Students are Living in the Future with Today's Technology*. Pew Internet and American Life Project <www.pew internet.org/pdfs/PIP_College_Report.pdf>.

Kaye, Barbara K. and Johnson, Thomas J. (1999) 'Research methodology: taming the cyber frontier: techniques for improving online surveys', *Social Science Computer Review*, 17 (3): 323–37.

Kitchin, Rob (1998) *Cyberspace: The World in the Wires*. Chichester: John Wiley.

Klingberg, Torkel (2009) *The Overflowing Brain: Information Overload and the Limits of Working Memory*. Oxford/New York: Oxford University Press.

Kollock, Peter and Smith, Marc (eds) (1999) *Communities in Cyberspace*. London/New York: Routledge.

Leander, K.M. and McKim, K.K. (2003) 'Tracing the everyday "sitings" of adolescents on the Internet: a strategic adaptation of ethnography across online and offline spaces', *Education, Communication, and Information*, 3 (2): 211–40.

Mann, Chris and Stewart, Fiona (2000) *Internet Communication and Qualitative Research: A Handbook for Researching Online*. London: Sage.

Mintz, Anne (ed.) (2002) *Web of Deception: Misinformation on the Internet*. Medford, NJ: CyberAge Books.

Nesbary, Dale K. (2000) *Survey Research and the World Wide Web*. Boston, MA: Allyn and Bacon.

Notess, Greg (1999–2006) *Search Engine Showdown* <searchengineshowdown.com>.

Pfaffenberger, Bryan (1997) *Official Microsoft Internet Explorer 4 Book*. Redmond, WA: Microsoft Press.

Sondermann, T.J. (2004–2006) *On Google Scholar* <schoogle.blogspot.com>.

Sullivan, Danny (ed.) (1997–2006) *Search Engine Watch* <www.searchenginewatch. com>.

Tapscott, Don (2009) *Grown up Digital*. New York: McGraw-Hill.

Tennant, Roy (ed.) (1990–2006) *Current Cites* <lists.webjunction.org/currentcites>.

Turkle, Sherry (1995) *Life on the Screen: Identity in the Age of the Internet*. New York: Simon & Schuster.

University of California, Berkeley, Library (2005) 'Finding information on the Internet: a tutorial' <www.lib.berkeley.edu/TeachingLib/Guides/Internet/FindInfo.html> (last updated: 31 August 2005).

Wikinews (2006) 'Congressional staff actions prompt Wikipedia investigation' <en.wikinews.org/wiki/Congressional_staff_actions_prompt_Wikipedia_investigation> 30 January 2006 (last updated: 9 February 2006).

Wimmer, Andreas and Lewis, Kevin (2010) 'Beyond and below racial homophily: ERG models of a friendship network documented on Facebook', *American Journal of Sociology*, 116 (2): 583–642.

Wyatt, Edward (2005) 'Writers sue Google, accusing it of copyright violation', *New York Times*, 21 September.

Index